HOW *To* BUILD *A* NATION

HOW *To* BUILD *A* NATION

R. KUMAR

Sarvatra
An imprint of Manjul Publishing House

Sarvatra
An imprint of Manjul Publishing House
• 2nd Floor, Usha Preet Complex,
42 Malviya Nagar, Bhopal 462 003 – India
• C-16, Sector 3, Noida, Uttar Pradesh 201301 – India
Website: www.manjulindia.com

How To Build A Nation

This edition first published in 2024

ISBN 978-93-5543-837-9

Printed and bound in India by Repro India Ltd.

How To Build A NATION?

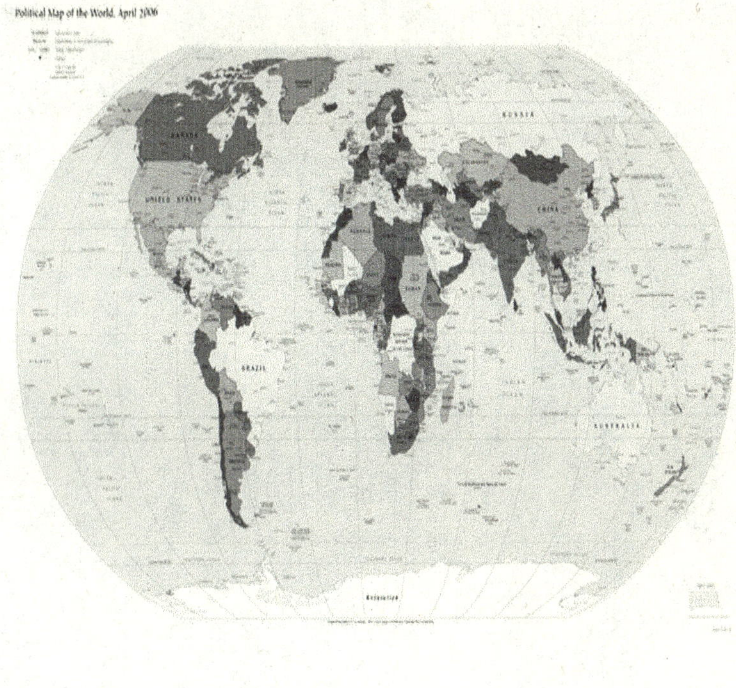

How To Build A NATION

An award ceremony for the "Jewels of India Award" and the "Certificate of Excellence," presented by the International Business Council, the International Institute of Education & Management, the Indian Solidarity Council, and the Economic Growth Foundation, to honor outstanding achievements and remarkable contributions in financial services and beyond.

Contents

B. ECONOMIC REFORMS

(A) Domestic Industrial Policies

(B) Import/Export Policies

(C) Increase in Revenue

(D) Reduction in Expenses

C. ADMINISTRATIVE/GOVERNMENT SECTOR – REFORMS

D. SOCIAL REFORMS

E. JUDICIAL REFORMS

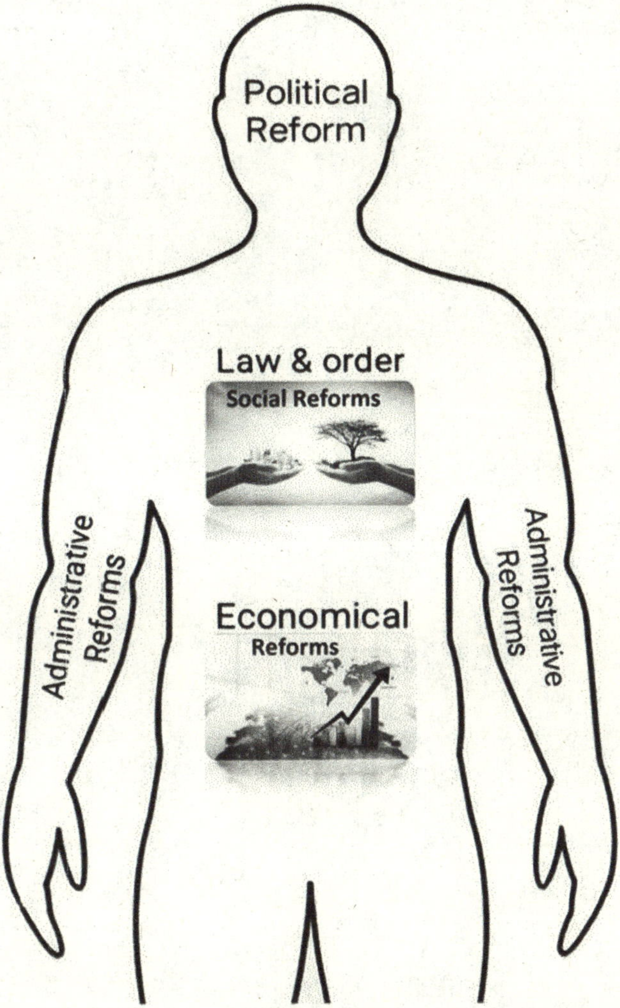
Political Reform
Law & order
Social Reforms
Administrative Reforms
Economical Reforms
Administrative Reforms

Preface

To build a strong and independent country that can do well in the world, we need to make five important changes:

1. **Political Changes:** We should improve how our government works.
2. **Economic Changes:** Our economy, or how we make and spend money, needs fixing.
3. **Administrative Changes:** A crucial sector, responsible for executing all policies and plans of the government effectively, needs improvement in its operations.
4. **Social Changes:** We must make our society better for everyone and ensure that everyone has a fair chance to succeed.
5. **Judicial Changes:** Our legal system needs improvement. We should ensure that justice is fair and that the law is followed correctly.

By making these five types of changes, our country can become powerful, self-reliant, and able to compete with other countries on the world stage. Building a strong nation is like building a strong house—it needs a strong foundation (political reforms), a well-functioning structure (economic reforms), a welcoming and safe environment (social reforms), and clear rules (judicial reforms) to ensure everything runs smoothly.

Further, the book isn't just about financial advice to help a country grow. It's also about the good things that make people proud of their country. When a country is strong, its people are united and work together to improve the nation. They choose to stay and work in their own country instead of going elsewhere. The book discusses emotions and their importance for a country. We will explore this further later.

This book has been written to offer special advice that can help a country remain strong and continue growing over time. It won't suggest actions that harm the environment or mistreat weaker countries. Instead, it will provide practical and smart ideas for the leaders of a country, whether they are currently in power or will be in the future. These ideas are easy to understand, regardless of age.

To put it simply, I will focus on broad plans that can improve a country's economy, as well as smaller plans for enhancing people's lives, maintaining peace, and ensuring harmony. All these plans are valuable and should be continuously implemented. However, we aim to create a system where work is done more efficiently and effectively. Time is money, and we want to avoid wasting it. To achieve this, we need to consider the bigger picture, how different elements work together, and how the government operates. This approach will make work faster and use fewer resources.

My next writing will explain how and what areas (that are directly or indirectly affected, either positively or negatively) must be addressed by the top-level ministries of the nation. These areas have been identified through core operations and a deep understanding of human behavior, with the possibility that scientific psychology might influence the workforce.

I wrote this book to offer valuable insights aimed at helping countries. I've strived to provide perspectives that you might not find elsewhere. Most books teach academic concepts.

For example, in a subject like "Business Management," books discuss what management means, the types of management, and the differences between good and bad management. But I want to go beyond that and help you understand more about how a country can improve.

How to Build a Nation is the fourth book by Mr. R. Kumar. Receiving appreciation from readers has motivated him to write on another diverse subject: The Build-up of a good nation.

The earlier books were on the business segment, covering the entire concept of running a business and the optimal use of time.

1. Chanakya of Modern Business Governance & Time Management
2. How to Manage - TIME?
3. How to Do - Business (To Eliminate Its Risks & Losses)?
4. How to Save - Marriage?

These books have proven to be valuable resources for various sectors, including industry professionals, entrepreneurs, government departments, and individuals alike.

Acknowledgments

In general, every new task involves three main factors:

1. Our own desires and circumstances, which give birth to our will.
2. Our efforts toward the goal, whether with or without the help of others.
3. Last but not least, the blessings of God. Without His mercy, we cannot move forward. It is important to note that God never allows our efforts to go to waste when they are done with good intentions. Despite our flaws, He never forgets to reward us for our good deeds.

So, first and foremost, I would like to thank and praise God Almighty for showering His blessings on me throughout my research work, enabling me to successfully complete this project. There were many times when I wanted to quit because I felt I didn't have enough information to continue writing. At those moments, I had two options: either give up and take a break or proceed with incomplete material for publication. This dilemma persisted until I had finished around 25 chapters of the book. If the supreme power hadn't given me the strength to persevere, this book would not have been possible in its current form.

I would also like to acknowledge the circumstances I have encountered throughout my life. I have realized that certain situations could have been better handled if they had been approached or presented differently, or if different actions had been taken at that time. These experiences led me to document all the situations I have faced and make a small effort toward the betterment of our society and, ultimately, our nation. I believe that sometimes discouraging moments can serve as motivation to do something extra and unique for society or a specific group of people. The key is to put in all your efforts to transform adverse situations into opportunities, both for yourself and others. I learned this from India's respected Prime Minister, Shri. Narendra Modi, who advised his fellow countrymen during the COVID-19 pandemic to view it as an opportunity rather than a setback. His inspiring message was embraced by Indian entrepreneurs, who proved themselves equally capable.

Finally, I am deeply grateful to my family for their love, patience, and prayers, which helped me complete this research work.

—R. Kumar

[B.Com Hons., FCA, DISA(ICA)]

Certified Arbitrator

About The Author

CA Rajeev Kumar Garg, a commerce graduate and Chartered Accountant by profession, with additional degrees in system audit and a certification course in ADR, has 29 years of experience in various capacities, including full-time employment, self-employed consulting, and entrepreneurship. He has applied his judgments, perceptions, self-life experiences, and insights from his career, both in commercial terms and as a citizen of a large nation, to write this book.

He was awarded the "Jewels of India" award in 2019 by the International Business Council and the Indian Solidarity Council for his remarkable role in financial matters. He also received a distinction in Business Management Accounting during his academic career. He was nominated and selected for the "International Royal Personality Award" in Bangkok by The Global Achievers Foundation, and for the "Mahatma Gandhi Leadership Award" by the NRI Welfare Society of India, presented at the British Parliament, House of Commons, London. Additionally, he was selected for the "Indian Achievers Award" 2022 by the Indian Achiever Forum, Delhi.

Mr. Garg's firm, Mak Grow Advisors, was shortlisted by "SiliconIndia," a leading business enterprise and technology magazine (US-India), as one of the "Best Consultations and Advisory Companies to Work For 2020."

The entire book is based solely on his thoughts, which he developed using his extrasensory brainpower to analyze individual countries' control and management systems, along with solutions to their issues. This work was accomplished while he simultaneously worked to earn a living due to limited resources. Before writing this national advisory, he also engaged in various diverse activities, including a trading business for personal experience. This business, started with minimal capital, has now developed into a significant conglomerate. While putting his business on autopilot as much as possible and continuing his job, he pursued studies by collecting data, meeting with people from different states and countries, comparing their systems, and analyzing their operations. Efforts have been made to cover all aspects contributing to a country's current status, without delving too deeply into each topic to ensure the book remains readable and engaging for readers.

In his opinion, if someone has the superior insight or intellect to understand other people's concerns, they can provide valuable advice. He is also the founder and advisor of a business advisory firm named Mak Grow Advisors, which specializes in advising business entities on their problems and dispute resolution. To learn more about the services offered, one may visit www.makgrowadvisors.com or call.

Reasons Behind Writing This Book

All the contents of this book support the interests of a nation, addressing both visible and invisible factors. The ruling party, at any given time, might be anyone in a country. However, all parties should be guided by their duties toward the nation, whether in power or not, and not merely enjoy the rights that come with their position in the administration.

We all have limited experience in running our own businesses or professions, facing tough competition within a limited scope. But managing a nation, with its diverse interests and responsibilities, presents a different level of challenge. To drive a country's growth in all areas requires a profound understanding, from grassroot issues to the latest techniques. The techniques and tips offered in this book are original and have been shaped by years of personal experience, addressing numerous challenges in social, cultural, and professional fields, as well as analyzing the operations of various entities and incidents encountered in routine life.

Economic Growth: When we talk about economic growth, there's more to it than just money. It involves using resources, making good decisions, and having a government that does the right things. Sometimes, two countries start with the same resources and strength, but over time, one does much better than the other. I wondered why this happened. I've seen situations where a ruling party claims they're doing everything right, but the results don't match. This book is my small contribution to all the nations that want to improve their systems and policies.

At a certain moment, when two countries have nearly equal resources, financial conglomerates, technical strength, or other infrastructure, a question comes to mind: Why, after some time, couldn't both run or progress parallelly? Why has a big difference emerged even though all the factors were almost equal at a certain time? Now, out of the two, one is doing very well and has reached a high level of success, while the other is not in the same position or has declined adversely. I analyzed those difficult situations when one says, "I was right as always, my every action was in the best interest of my country, and even today, my way of running this country is better than the others." In support of their opinion, the ruling party generally quotes several examples or other cases in various media. This effort is a small contribution to all those nations who have the same feeling and have a keen desire to do away with the shortcomings of the system in every field and are also interested in improving their respective policies, strategies, and so on.

I was also inspired to write this book by a common question: Why do some countries lag in economic growth or other areas compared to others? This made me dig deeper and find out what's wrong with the way countries operate. I wanted to find solutions to help these nations and their citizens. Many countries face problems like inflation, food shortages, financial troubles, and even internal conflicts.

FAQs

Q1. What does this book tell the reader?

Ans. This book takes care of every factor, regardless of its size. Sometimes small things become game changers in a field. Don't ignore the invisible effects of your actions or policies. Running a country successfully is no less than fighting a war for its government, where a particular party either loses or gains power due to its actions during its tenure, similar to winning or losing a war.

A. Political Reforms

Chapter 1

Approach of the Ruling Government

This is the pivotal facet upon which the entire spectrum of advancement, vision for the nation's long-term future, state of internal and external harmony, and social equilibrium of a country profoundly relies. Numerous elements ascertain the progress of any nation. Broadly delineating, when a ruling party makes choices in favor of the nation's well-being rather than merely gathering votes and gives preference to integrity, intellect, diligence, and equality over casteism, factionalism, and nationalism, then undoubtedly that nation sustains a positive standing compared to others embracing a contrary approach. Here, in a broader context, we can explain the strategies of a ruling party in two manners:

1. Vision Towards the Nation's Long-Term Interest
2. Short-Term Vision Driven by Self-Interest

First Approach

In the first category of governance, all the divisions of their ministry, bureaucracy, personnel, etc., are instructed to execute all actions with a vision of long-term gains, even if the immediate results do not hold significant propaganda or serve as instant remedies for the populace. Steps are undertaken while retaining their constructive essence, and gradually, people recognize the merits of these policies. Here, the party's approach is to foster the nation and its citizens. In later times, the fruition of these policies might materialize, with the next or forthcoming generations relishing the fruits of today's efforts.

Even in diplomatic relations with other countries, they maintain stringent measures that safeguard their industries, populace, and so forth. This becomes evident in our daily lives when certain import or export policies undergo frequent modifications to protect our own commercial sectors.

The assertion of the party's vote bank cannot be entirely disregarded. It is noteworthy that such parties predominantly make decisions, formulate laws, establish system procedures, implement these strategies, and maintain a healthy equilibrium between revenue and expenditure, or rather savings and capital expenditure, all while considering the optimal level of borrowing.

It remains hard work for such a government, which works for the long-term sustainability of the nation, as people do not understand the benefits of such policies in the early stages. However, the impact of these policies comes to light after a few months or years. Now it becomes the duty of the people to take things the right way as well as in their own interest. No doubt, opposition parties take it as an opportunity to condemn the ruling party by gaining public support against such policies whose benefits do not seem immediately apparent. If such is the scenario, the ruling party loses its confidence to implement more such acts in the interest of the public, whose benefit the public would gain in the future. It has been observed that there remain chances of internal conflicts within the ruling party itself when some members have opinions against the party's policies and favor initiating those acts which have an immediate effect on the public.

> "Erroneous decisions made by a government can plunge the nation into darkness, while wise choices illuminate its path to global acclaim."

Second Approach

If a government adopts this type of vision, it may not prove to be fruitful for the nation. The ruling government might undertake fewer tasks that benefit the nation and focus more on actions that cater to their own vote bank, steering the nation's course for long-term gain. Such a government may offer "sweet sauce" through their announcements, which ultimately proves detrimental to the public.

The next generation or future governments will face various interlocked problems as a result. The external status of the country could be adversely affected, including financial debts, weakened international standing, exploitation, and internal interference. The country's external standing might also suffer significantly. Therefore, when the country is governed by such a party, it falls upon the citizens to adopt a far-sighted outlook and take necessary steps to emancipate the country from their control.

SUMMARY

In the grand scheme of things, the perspective adopted by the governing party plays a crucial role in a country's progress. Many factors contribute to a nation's development, and the decisions related to these factors sketch the path of its advancement. A forward-looking approach that prioritizes the nation over self-interest propels the country to remarkable heights on the global stage. As I have already clarified the role of citizens above, I would like to emphasize once more that people, whether they are affiliated with the ruling party or the opposition, should comprehend such policies with the right perspective and impartiality.

Chapter 2

Policies and Plans of the Ruling Government

The way the ruling government approaches things matters greatly, and the different policies in various areas also significantly affect a country's progress or lack thereof compared to others. When a particular government is in power, all activities are carried out based on set policies approved by the majority of members in Parliament. A nation's progress aligns with the effectiveness of these policies. Each government outlines actions for different parts of the country's economy. Although it's not possible to describe all of them here, let's touch on some of the major ones:

- Financial Sector Policies
- Industrial Sector Policies
- Agricultural Sector Policies
- Foreign Policies, including International Trade
- Defense Policies
- Law & Order Policies
- Social Welfare Policies that impact citizens directly & many others.

The above examples significantly impact a country's economy, and many other policies also influence economic development positively or negatively. Strong policies contribute to a better nation.

Prominent business leaders eagerly await the government's announcements regarding changes in business policies, and they adjust their expansion plans accordingly. In the business world, factors like the feasibility of business operations, strategic vision, industry infrastructure support (whether manufacturing or service-oriented), protection against cheap imports, access to finance, geographical or other subsidies, and profits after tax (PAT) are all considered along with loyalty to the nation.

In an interview with Mr. Gautam Adani, the third richest person in Asia, which aired on India Today's TV Channel on December 28, 2022, the role of government policies was explained clearly and in detail. Mr. Adani discussed India's economic growth since its independence, spanning 75 years under various political parties. He mentioned that out of these 75 years, the country reached a one trillion USD economy in the first 58 years, a two trillion USD economy in the subsequent 12 years, and a three trillion USD economy in just five years. This underscores the significant role of government policies in shaping a nation's destiny, without which a country could remain stagnant or even decline.

Out of the numerous, these policies should cover the broader spectrum of economic development, including manufacturing, agriculture, and service sectors. Additionally, the socio-economic sector is equally crucial. Any governing body should consistently focus on these areas despite the challenges within the country. Economic growth is essential for a country and its people to be recognized globally.

Government laws and industrial policies should support the manufacturing, agriculture, and service sectors.

They should be industry-friendly and consider aspects like labor, transportation, taxes, and import/export policies. To formulate a country's business policies, studying successful policies from other countries could be beneficial and adopted where suitable.

SUMMARY

There's no harm in each household engaging in manufacturing, whether on a large or small scale. The ruling government, during its term, must recognize its responsibility to formulate policies in every domain that propel the nation to new heights. Just like China, becoming a manufacturing hub can significantly boost a country's economic growth.

Chapter 3

Follow the Plans of Developed Countries

It can be beneficial to follow the policies of countries that have experienced high GDP growth. Instead of causing harm, adopting their strategies might be advantageous. To do this, we can study and analyze the growth rates of those nations over a few years. We can then try to implement similar strategies in our country while ensuring we don't compromise our own principles, goals, or other values.

We might not be able to replicate everything exactly, so we can modify the strategies to fit our own circumstances. While adopting these policies, we should deeply consider our core values, principles, and the unseen challenges that might arise in the future due to imitating other countries.

The size of the population, the ratio of skilled to unskilled workers, literacy rates, the existing status of employment in the home country, and various other factors need to be studied, appraised, and analyzed prior to planning or implementing the strategies carried out by a developed country.

This kind of adoption is often observed in the technology sector and can be quite effective. It's also recommended for long-term policies. The key is to strike a balanced approach between our own values and those of other nations.

"Principle of a balanced approach between our values and others' should be taken care of."

SUMMARY

Innovations are unlimited. No one is complete. God has bestowed some uniqueness on everyone. Implementing a few successful ideas from others for our own benefit does not harm anyone.

Chapter 4

Strategy of International Relations

If a country's plans are right and diplomatic, it can grow significantly, get help from the whole world, and be in a good position globally. When a country is firm and has good relationships with others, it becomes important in groups like the United Nations. This group aims to make the world better, keep peace between countries, help weaker countries avoid unfair treatment, and provide assistance during natural disasters. Other groups like NATO, WHO, and the World Bank have similar goals. When a country is strong in these groups, it helps them when they need it, makes it easier to trade with other countries, and allows them to share knowledge and learn new things.

Governments need to make plans about dealing with other countries that help both sides, increase production for export, obtain needed resources, support the military, and facilitate their people's ability to travel to richer countries.

When one country allows another to bring in goods, it can significantly help the second country grow.

In the world of international relations, having the right approach is like steering a ship in the right direction. If a country's plans are smart and well-thought-out, it can lead to growth and support from other countries. Just like a ship with a strong anchor and well-built sails can navigate rough waters, a nation with a clear stance and positive friendships can face global challenges with confidence.

Being part of groups like the United Nations, NATO, WHO, and the World Bank is like joining a team of countries that all want the world to be a better place. It's like being in a club where everyone works together for peace and helps each other. When a country is respected in these groups, it's like having many friends who can lend a hand when times get tough.

Numerous organizations exist on the international platform, representing the unity of member countries towards achieving common goals, maintaining peace, and ensuring the combined growth of all. Sharing a common platform fosters friendly relations, and when such alliances happen at national levels, they create significant mutual benefits, support, and unity among those countries. For others, this strength conveys a message of supremacy in the world.

No doubt, the respective country that hosts such summits has to incur significant expenditure and make high-profile arrangements for the delegations participating in the event. Opposition parties also leave no stone unturned in criticizing the ruling party over the heavy financial expenditures, expecting short-term benefits. Consequently, the parties that vocally oppose the spending often succeed in attracting public support, while the ruling party bears the brunt of public defamation.

When discussing the G20 Summits, the Presidency is responsible for coordinating the G20 agenda in consultation with other members and in response to developments in the global economy.

When governments make plans for dealing with other countries, they should think long-term. It's like planning for a journey that will benefit both sides. By working together, countries can trade things they're good at making, help each other during tough times, and even learn from each other's strengths.

Hosting events like the Olympics or other sports events is good for any nation to attract global attention and foster familiarity among nations. However, when a summit is conducted at the international level, it results in economic benefits, peace at borders, and sends a message of a strong image to other countries.

During tough times, just as people try to get along despite differences, countries too need to be diplomatic. This means they should talk things out and find common ground. It's like how friends help each other solve problems. This approach can prevent conflicts from escalating and even help settle disputes between other countries.

SUMMARY

Remember the saying, "To make a friend takes time, but to make an enemy might not take long." Just as making friends is important, it's crucial to build good relationships with other countries. The wisdom of thinkers like Indian philosopher Chanakya can guide nations in maintaining peaceful relations with everyone.

Chapter 5

Relationships With Rich Economies

Maintaining a nation's independence, defense capabilities, self-esteem, and national values are essential. But it's also important for countries to have positive connections with wealthier nations. These rich nations have a lot of money, resources, and expertise in technology. Even if there are some differences, these differences shouldn't get in the way of having good relationships and doing business with them. This helps our own industries, whether they make things, offer services, or trade goods. They are also equally important for a nation that contributes to the economic growth of a country.

It's not about favoring rich countries over others. All countries, big or small, play a part in a nation's economic growth. Think of it like this: if one country has $1,000 and another has $10,000, it doesn't make sense for the $1,000 country to create unnecessary problems with the richer one. Sometimes, issues are brought up with wealthy countries that don't really affect our nation. These issues might actually harm us more than help.

This context is also supported by a news article published in the "*Punjab Kesari*" Hindi newspaper on 23-12-2022 (Page 9, Column 5) where Mr. Arvind Pangaria, Ex-Deputy Chairman of the Planning Commission, expressed that breaking business relations is not advisable, even if the situation on the border is tense at that time.

Diplomatic Ties

Even if keeping good relations is hard, diplomatic connections shouldn't be given up. Even with countries we don't get along with, we should keep talking. It's about helping people, even if it's just a little bit, and showing kindness even behind the scenes. This can win over the people of another country and make them like us more. Then, they might want to buy things from our country, which helps our businesses become well-known globally.

SUMMARY

We should work hard to maintain good business relationships, especially with wealthier countries. But remember, this shouldn't go against our own values, our people, our resources, or our industries. It's like making friends who have more than us – we can benefit from their strengths while staying true to who we are.

चीन के साथ व्यापार संबंधों को तोड़ना नुकसानदायक हो सकता है: पनगढ़िया

नई दिल्ली, 22 दिसम्बर (प.स.): सीमा पर आक्रामक रुख दिखा रहे चीन के साथ व्यापार संबंधों को तोड़ने की मांगों के बीच नीति आयोग के पूर्व उपाध्यक्ष अरविंद पनगढ़िया ने कहा कि मौजूदा स्थिति में पेइचिंग के साथ व्यापार संबंधों को खत्म करने का मतलब भारत की संभावित आर्थिक वृद्धि का बलिदान करना होगा ।

उन्होंने कहा कि इसके बजाए तो भारत को अपने व्यापार का विस्तार करने के लिए ब्रिटेन और यूरोपीय संघ समेत अन्य देशों के साथ मुक्त व्यापार समझौते करने के प्रयास करने चाहिएं।

पनगढ़िया ने कहा, ''इस स्थिति में चीन के साथ व्यापारिक जंग छेड़ने का मतलब होगा हमारी संभावित वृद्धि के साथ समझौता करना। इसकी (सीमा पर तनाव) प्रतिक्रिया में कार्रवाई करना उपयुक्त नहीं होगा।''

कोलंबिया विश्वविद्यालय में अर्थशास्त्र के प्रोफैसर पनगढ़िया ने कहा कि दोनों देश व्यापार प्रतिबंध जैसे कदम उठा सकते हैं लेकिन 17000 अरब डॉलर की अर्थव्यवस्था (चीन) में 3000 अरब डॉलर की अर्थव्यवस्था (भारत) को नुकसान पहुंचाने की क्षमता कहीं अधिक होगी। उन्होंने कहा कि अमरीका जैसी बड़ी अर्थव्यवस्था भी चीन या रूस के खिलाफ प्रतिबंध लगाने में उतनी सफल नहीं रही है।

पनगढ़िया ने कहा, ''हमें अगले दशक के लिए भारत की वृद्धि की शानदार संभावनाओं का लाभ उठाते हुए अर्थव्यवस्था को जितना ज्यादा संभव हो उतना बड़ा करने पर ध्यान देना चाहिए। एक बार हम तीसरी सबसे बड़ी अर्थव्यवस्था बन जाएंगे तो हमारे प्रतिबंध का असर भी ज्यादा होगा।''

Chapter 6

Maintaining Peace at the Border

For long-term steady growth, disturbances at international borders or with neighboring countries should be at zero level. The presence of disturbances in these regions not only diverts the attention of governments from internal agendas of peace, growth, and social welfare but also demotivates the people within these countries from their regular pursuits. The repercussions of such situations go beyond mere military and political aspects, adversely impacting economies and societies.

It is commonly observed that nations facing the possibility of conflict experience a significant downturn in their economic performance compared to their previous records. This downturn happens by default. Although the borders are managed by the military forces and the high command of that country, the general populace also becomes preoccupied with the tensions, diverting their energy and attention away from their usual activities.

In such scenarios, the pursuit of growth-oriented strategies becomes an afterthought, as the nation's resources and attention are absorbed by resolving disputes or preparing for potential conflict. The consequences ripple through various sectors, including markets, trade, manufacturing, agriculture, and services, all of which suffer adverse effects. This situation, even if for a shorter time, sets the nation back for a number of years, and the GDP of that period declines drastically or even turns negative.

If we examine the history of the world, we find that none of the countries involved in such disputes could gain a better position after the war for several years. The volume of such losses may be higher or lesser for the involved countries but cannot be ignored. Huge expenses and resources have to be incurred for the deployment of security forces. In pursuing chapters, investment in weapons and other defense materials will be described.

Apart from the above-mentioned visible adverse effects, invisible ones also occur. For example, when all countries were progressing at a smooth and steady pace, such incidents divided the world broadly into 2-3 parts, creating factions based on individual opinions or affiliations with the warring countries. These types of alliances hamper collective growth and progress or in dealing with terrorist activities in the world. Such a situation shouldn't arise; otherwise, it takes countries back a number of years in terms of their growth.

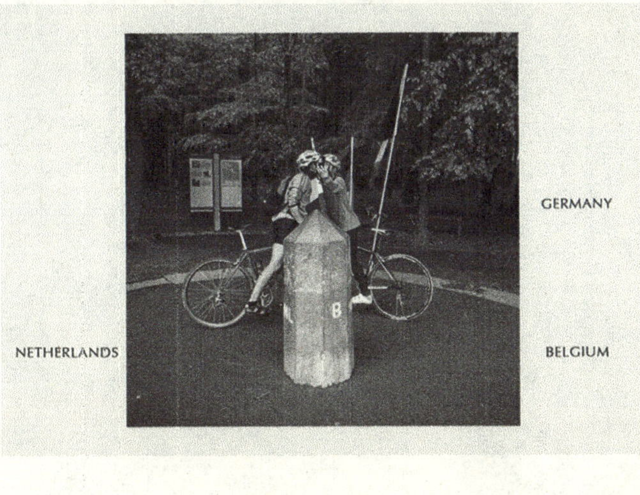

SUMMARY

In summary, maintaining peace along borders is paramount for sustainable growth and well-being. The repercussions of border conflicts extend beyond military and political realms, affecting economies, societies, and global cooperation. To secure lasting progress, nations must prioritize peaceful resolutions over conflicts that invariably disrupt growth trajectories.

Chapter 7

Constructive Role of Opposition or Political Parties

Opposition parties play a very important role in keeping a country peaceful and well-managed. The internal peace of a nation is maintained due to the right approach to opposition. Their actions and behavior matter a lot. When opposition parties work in a helpful and constructive way, it improves the country's internal affairs. However, sometimes they make a lot of noise even when the ruling party is doing the right things. This can cause problems in how the country is run, confuse the public, and waste time for the nation and its people. This can even happen during important meetings like the Lok Sabha or Vidhan Sabha sessions, where important decisions and laws are supposed to be discussed and kept for approval by the respective houses.

Opposition parties act as a check on the ruling party. If the ruling party is planning to do something that could harm the country, the opposition steps in to stop them. But the opposition shouldn't always criticize the ruling party, especially when the decisions are good for the country. The ruling party also must answer questions and explain things to the opposition. However, they should do it in a way that the opposition can't keep asking the same questions over and over again, wasting everyone's time.

In an example from India during a parliamentary session, an opposition party blamed the ruling party for allowing another country (China) to occupy their country's land. The ruling party continuously denies such allegations and says that not even an inch of the country's land has been taken. These debates have occurred numerous times within Parliament and outside of it.

Had the ruling party shown proof in the Lok Sabha that no land was taken, the opposition might have stopped talking about it. This would have saved a lot of time and energy for the political leaders and the entire population who heard or saw this news in the media.

A strong democracy benefits from a healthy opposition that provides checks and balances to the ruling party. Opposition parties can serve as a voice for different perspectives and ideas, promoting a robust exchange of viewpoints that leads to better decision-making. When opposition parties engage in constructive criticism, it forces the ruling party to carefully consider their actions and policies. This back-and-forth debate within the political landscape contributes to the growth and development of a nation.

However, a delicate balance needs to be maintained. While opposition parties have the responsibility to question and challenge the government, **they should also recognize when to support initiatives that are genuinely beneficial for the nation.** Overly aggressive opposition tactics can create gridlock and hinder progress. **Similarly, the ruling party should respond to opposition concerns with transparency and facts,** avoiding unnecessary political theatrics that waste valuable legislative time.

SUMMARY

Ultimately, a nation benefits when opposition parties act as responsible watchdogs, raising valid concerns and ensuring that the government remains accountable to its citizens. A constructive opposition can foster a more inclusive and effective governance process, leading to the overall advancement of the country.

Chapter 8

Alignment Between Centre & States

Although political parties may differ between the central government and state governments, it is important for them to work together for the benefit of the nation.

Let's begin with the idea that when the ruling party at the national level doesn't have much in common with the parties in different states, there's a big chance for conflicts, disagreements, blaming each other, or not cooperating in making decisions or policies that are good for the country. Otherwise, a lot of time, effort, and resources - both human and other kinds - are wasted in arguing or resolving these conflicts. This doesn't just waste the time of the government or different departments, but also of ordinary people who pay attention through social media, news channels, and other sources.

Examples are when a Prime Minister visits a state governed by the opposition party & issue has been framed over the security arrangements of the Prime Minister or when opposition parties in some states oppose the implementation of the GST and agricultural bills. Many times, the country's President or Prime Minister is from one political party while the Chief Minister of a state is from the opposition party. In these cases, even when the President or Prime Minister visits the state, they don't share the same platform with the Chief Minister. These joint platforms are meant to benefit the people of that state. Similarly, when new policies or taxes are introduced, the central and state authorities don't always work together to make these policies successful.

This lack of alignment between the central and state governments has several disadvantages. It can lead to inefficiencies,. misunderstandings and even create opportunities for other countries to interfere in our country's internal matters.

Collaboration between the central government and state governments is crucial for the smooth functioning and development of a country. When leaders from different nation, it sends a strong message of unity and purpose. This united front not only ensures effective policy implementation but also strengthens the country's position on the international stage.

The lack of alignment between central and state governments can lead to confusion among citizens, as differing policies and decisions might create disparities between regions. It also impedes the efficient utilization of resources, as coordination becomes challenging. When central and state governments work in harmony, it fosters an environment of mutual trust and respect, leading to more transparent governance.

For instance, when states and the central government cooperate in implementing policies such as tax reforms or economic measures, the impact is more comprehensive and effective. This coordination minimizes confusion among businesses and citizens, allowing them to adapt to changes more smoothly.

SUMMARY

In summary, when political parties set aside their differences and collaborate for the betterment of the nation, it not only benefits the citizens but also fortifies the overall resilience and progress of the country. Such unity acts as a barrier against external interference and fosters a sense of belonging and purpose among the population.

Chapter 9

Change of Political Parties and Its Impact on Administration

Periodical changes in any ruling Government, whether at the level of local authorities, State Government, or Central, are always welcome and have numerous benefits for the public as well as for the Nation. No Government is 100% perfect in all matters of running a nation. With such changes, the best qualities of different governments can be utilized for society. Moreover, public interest is also evident whenever elections are held, as people vote according to the performance of the past Government.

Up to the above-mentioned facts, which are known to all, there arises a grey area either intentionally or by default, which needs to be taken care of with one's sixth sense. Why I am commenting on this topic will become clear in the upcoming paragraphs.

In all the Government departments where, political posts are required to be filled, such as Chairman, Trustee, Consultants, Advisory Committees, or even in Rajya Sabha, the winning party always prefers to appoint their own men who might be supporters or party workers to these positions. Now, this raises the question of whether these appointed personnel are really competent to capture such decision-making posts.

If they are, then there are no objections, but on the contrary, if they are not, what would happen to the activities of that particular department? In a commonly accepted principle, an individual's qualifications, age limit, experience, etc., are judged through written tests as well as interviews whenever recruitment is required in a particular department. Had it been an open recruitment process for such departments, would such appointees have succeeded in the competition? This is a major question that should be considered.

Both state and central governments directly control a number of government departments, cooperative banks, and other welfare schemes. These appointees are supposed to be decision-makers in their respective offices. If these appointees have little to no experience but are responsible for decision-making in government schemes involving national money, it may result in various problems.

These changes affect the working of that organization in several ways:

(a) **No Work in the Last Year:** In the final year of a ruling party's term, constructive work or planning may be avoided out of fear of elections. All controlling authorities may only perform routine work, self-interest work, or engage in propaganda for the ruling party's election.

(b) **Non-Deserving Candidates:** It is often seen that the above-mentioned posts are filled without matching the person's capabilities with the work. Even posts of Chairpersons are sometimes filled not through open public selection but by individuals who contributed to the ruling party's victory. If the newly appointed person is not competent, the progress of that department may be hindered.

We can correlate this with the following example:

Suppose a father has two different businesses managed by his two sons. If he suddenly switches their duties, both may not work smoothly.

(a) **Learning Time:** New appointees need time to understand their roles, which can delay decisions and progress.

(b) **Delayed Problem-Solving:** Old issues often linger until there is strong pressure to address them.

(c) **Unnecessary Transfers:** Officers are sometimes transferred without a real need, causing disruptions.

Frequent changes in government departments, such as in the police and various ministries, can have broader implications. While changes bring new perspectives and fresh ideas, they can also lead to disruptions, inefficiencies, and a loss of institutional memory. When personnel changes occur too frequently, the continuity of policies and projects may be compromised.

One example of this is the frequent transfers of officials, even when they were recently moved or when there is no logical reason for the transfer. This constant shifting can undermine the stability and effectiveness of departments. It is important to strike a balance between introducing new talent and maintaining stability in key positions.

SUMMARY

While changing governments brings new opportunities, it's essential to consider the potential drawbacks they might bring. Striking a balance between political appointments and merit-based selections can ensure that the government machinery operates efficiently and effectively, benefiting the nation as a whole. Open discussions about these challenges are crucial to finding the best way forward.

Chapter 10

Opportunities in Accordance with Capabilities

In countries where governance isn't managed well, some common problems arise. Many government opportunities tend to favor close friends, supporters, or those with strong connections. This happens when someone is chosen not because they're the best fit for the job but because they have the right connections. In such cases, the person chosen might not have the necessary skills for the job.

When jobs are given based on connections rather than merit, the people in those positions often lack the skills needed for the job. If these positions were filled through open competition, more capable individuals would step up. They would bring fresh ideas and work in the best interests of society and the nation.

I've faced this issue myself, and I've heard from many others who have faced similar problems despite being highly qualified. They were held back because they didn't have the right connections in that department.

For any government plan to succeed, the integrity of the people executing it is crucial. A well-thought-out plan can lose its value if those responsible for carrying it out don't do their duty honestly and compromise their ethics and morals.

This often happens due to bribery, corruption, or pressure from influential people.

Individuals or teams working on plan implementation might leak information or act in favor of the other party instead of their own department. The original purpose of the plan gets defeated because of people pursuing their self-interest. These individuals can be government staff, officers, politicians, or anyone within the government machinery.

There are many examples of such situations, and you may recall incidents from the past where government actions were compromised due to corruption or lack of integrity. An example in India is the demonetization process, which faced challenges due to the actions of some government employees, bank staff, or manipulators in the public. Similarly, investigations, searches, or seizures conducted by various government agencies like Income Tax, GST/VAT, Customs, etc., can fail if the team neglects important aspects because of corruption or lack of intelligence.

These issues have far-reaching consequences and impact the effectiveness of government actions. It's essential to address them to ensure a fair and just society.

SUMMARY

Honesty is particularly important for those responsible for carrying out any government action.

Chapter 11

Ban on Hate Speeches

If there are existing laws, they should be reviewed and updated as necessary to address emerging issues.

Yes, I am referring to the laws that regulate hate speech in a country. Obviously, these laws should apply to everyone, every place, and every type of media. A wrongful act or speech by an individual can be easily identified and held accountable. The principle of awareness generally applies here and should be emphasized by the government to ensure that people understand these laws and their associated punishments. Proper laws, along with public knowledge about them, address the issue comprehensively.

Another responsibility lies with the media, whose influence significantly impacts the public. Constructive contributions from any type of media help maintain peace within a country. On the contarary, irresponsible media coverage can lead to disturbances, riots, and divisions based on caste, religion, and locality. The negative consequences of such actions are evident and can sometimes even lead to the division of a country.

In simple terms, I broadly define the types of media as follows:

1. Readable Media

People come to know what is happening at a certain place or a certain time through this media, and this was the first way news circulation started in ancient times. Newspapers, magazines, pamphlets, books, text messages, or any type of paper come within the purview of this segment. To have awareness, to the extent of its coverage, about the happenings in a specified area, is utilized by people. The involvement of other people, such as press reporters, editors, or publishing houses, is present in all the news before it is printed, compared to other media where viewers or listeners have a direct approach to the speakers.

Why I am describing all this, or some may say that I am going out of the topic, is because this process has its own features in the circulation of news and perhaps in the interest of the nation as well. While a press reporter is going to publish a piece of news, they have to pass such news through many hands, including their own, editors, and others. By default, a filtration process gets started, and the impact of such publication on the public cannot be ignored. Part of the content that may prove hard on the public or can spread hate elements is generally modified before its publishing. *Efforts are being made to soften the news without changing its original purpose or sometimes are ignored.* This exercise contributes to maintaining things in a softened manner. Secondly, not everyone has a habit of reading or has the time to read the whole news. These factors contribute to readable media having a lesser impact than others.

2. Listenable/Audible Media

It is also a traditional way of reaching the news or other information to the people of a nation. Until videos were accessible to the masses, this media was used effectively. In the present time, this media has lost its importance, particularly in urban areas, but hasn't been fully eliminated, particularly in rural areas. A gramophone and radio are examples of such media. The benefits of this media are nearly equal to those of readable media concerning the impact of the news. Before announcing any news, a filtration of the content is generally made before its broadcast. Additionally, people do not have as much capacity for just listening compared to the next defined media, which creates interest with the addition of one feature: viewing.

3. Video and Audio Media

Yes, this is the new invention of the current scenario and far ahead of TV channels, which are also part of this segment. The use of this media has left far behind the above two ways, which require some effort, whether physical or mental, to read or listen. Although listening happens simultaneously with the running of the video, making it enjoyable and interesting for everyone, this is the reason people from almost every sphere of life prefer this media over the above two. Social media is another added feature of this era where everyone has the right to express their views in public.

So now, the effect of such hate speeches or similar content impacts more in this media compared to others. They spread quickly among the public, and the reactions of people come to light.

In a country, all types of incidents continue to happen. Some have minor effects, while others may ruin peaceful circumstances, leading to riots or groupism. The internal strength that should come from within for the growth of the country is lost due to these agitations, dharnas, and disingenuous demands from various communities. This media works too quickly to reach a large part of society.

Even the most sensitive issues reach the public at the same pace, regardless of any filtration intended to serve the nation's interests, allowing people to act based on their own judgment or under the influence of their leaders. Sometimes matters are not so sensitive but are presented in a particular manner due to personal interest or other reasons. This occurs because they are not presented by an organized sector but rather by a very common person.

The name of this media is "social," but sometimes it creates unsocial elements in society. To control this, there should be some regulations. One possible approach could be to balance individual freedom with the constraints of such laws, but many times it is used to gain unlawful benefits.

Chapter 12

Proposing a Screening Committee for Political Parties

People often find themselves bewildered or confused when confronted with entirely contradictory statements from different political parties, especially when the response to assigning blame boils down to a binary choice of "Yes" or "No." In such situations, a definitive and transparent answer from a reputable authority could put an end to the controversy.

I have observed prolonged disputes when opposition parties accuse the ruling government of a neighboring country occupying a portion of our nation's land, while the ruling party vehemently refutes these allegations, asserting, as in courtroom proceedings, that "it is incorrect" and emphatically adding that "not even an inch of our land has been seized by the enemy country." Surprisingly, neither side presents any tangible evidence to support their claims during this protracted period, leaving the arena open for an ongoing cycle of accusations and counter-accusations.

This recurring scenario unfolds in various settings, whether within the chambers of the Lok Sabha, the Rajya Sabha, or during press conferences. The press, electronic media, and social media, among other outlets, consistently play their roles whenever such conflicting statements resurface.

In the interest of the public and the pursuit of a more transparent and accountable political landscape, the idea of establishing a Screening Committee for all political parties has been put forth. This committee's primary function is to provide an unadulterated view of the functioning of the government and to filter political statements and blame games among parties. This proposal aims to outline the role, functions, advantages, and potential disadvantages of such a committee.

Role and Functions of the Committee

Transparency in Government Activities

The primary role of the Screening Committee is to act as a mirror reflecting the activities of the ruling party, both at the state and national levels. It will maintain a comprehensive record of all government actions, evaluating their alignment with the nation's interests. This will ensure that the public has access to unfiltered information about the government's performance.

Filtering Political Statements

One of the critical functions of the Committee is to screen the statements issued by political parties and their mutual blame games. This committee will analyze these statements objectively and present an unbiased view to the public. By doing so, it will help reduce the dissemination of politically motivated and misleading information.

Advantages

Time and Energy Savings

The Screening Committee will enable citizens to save time

and energy that might otherwise be wasted on unproductive political debates and discussions. By presenting an accurate and unfiltered view of government activities, the public can focus on more constructive pursuits.

Enhanced Informed Decision-Making

Many individuals have limited and often biased sources of information. The Committee will provide a reliable and impartial source of information to help citizens make informed decisions about their political choices. This will reduce the risk of misleading information influencing voters.

Increased Productivity

As the public dedicates less time to contentious political discussions and more time to their personal and professional activities, overall productivity in the country is likely to increase. This can contribute to the nation's progress and prosperity.

Disadvantages

Independence and Bias

There may be concerns about the Committee's independence and potential bias in interpreting political statements and government actions. Ensuring the Committee remains impartial and free from any undue influence is crucial.

Financial Costs

Establishing and maintaining such a committee would involve financial expenses. Funding sources and budget allocation would need to be carefully considered to prevent any financial burden on the state.

Overreach and Privacy Concerns

There is a fine line between monitoring government activities and potentially infringing on individuals' privacy. Striking a balance between transparency and privacy is a challenge that needs to be addressed.

SUMMARY

In conclusion, the establishment of a Screening Committee for all political parties presents a promising concept to enhance political transparency and reduce the spread of misinformation. To realize its benefits, careful planning and consideration of potential disadvantages are essential. Such a committee can contribute to a more informed, engaged, and productive citizenry, fostering a healthier political landscape.

B. Economic Reforms

(A) Domestic Industrial Policies.

(B) Import/Export Policies.

(C) Increase Of Revenue.

(D) Reduction In Expenses.

(A) DOMESTIC INDUSTRIAL POLICIES

Chapter 13

Save Our Industry

Our industries are like the heart of our country's economy. They create jobs, bring in money, and help us stand strong. With the rise of the internet, things have changed a lot. Now, people can buy and sell things online from all around the world. This can be good, but it can also make things tough for our local businesses and in making the state an industrial hub.

The government's efforts to set up industrial hubs also require continuous protection. With the rise of e-business, it becomes more crucial for every nation to safeguard their industries from the changing business scenario and equip themselves to compete in the international bazaar or market. While e-business might affect manufacturing to an extent, its impact on a country's trading business is more significant. Rules and regulations that govern e-business activities need to be regulated, defined, and fall under the scope of different taxation statutes of a country.

In my opinion, e-business should enter from the second stage of distribution, not directly from the manufacturer. If they start from the first level where they directly purchase from the manufacturer, it could lead to the closure of small trading businesses or shops. This would result in a lot of people involved in small-scale trading losing their jobs.

Imagine if big online companies started buying things straight from the factories. This might make things cheaper for them, but it could make it really hard for the small shops where we usually buy things. If these small shops close down, many people who work there might lose their jobs, and that wouldn't be good for our country.

SUMMARY

So, it's important for the government to make sure that while online business grows, our own industries and jobs stay safe. They need to make rules that ensure everyone plays fair and that our local shops and businesses can still compete. This way, we can enjoy the benefits of the internet while keeping our own economy strong.

Chapter 14

World's Factory/Manufacturing Hub: Like That of China

Also referred to as "*Vinirman Kendra*" in Hindi.

Manufacturing involves different processes that transform raw materials into finished products. This can happen through machines, electricity, people working manually, or a combination of these methods. All of these methods transform raw materials into final products that we can use or into parts that are used to make bigger things.

For a country's economy to grow significantly, it needs a lot of money invested, called capital, and it also needs to make things efficiently and quickly. Making more things than needed is good because extra things can be sold to other countries, which brings in more money. This helps the country's economy and creates jobs for people. It also makes sure that the country's resources, like materials and tools, are used well.

Understanding what manufacturing means shows how important it is for a country's progress. The more a country makes things, the stronger its position in the world becomes. Without manufacturing, a country might not do as well as other leading countries.

Economically strong countries make a lot of the world's

manufactured goods. Some countries have figured out how to do this, and it's not just about having a lot of money or resources. The government's role, where the country's leaders make important decisions, is very important. Other factors like where the country is located, how easy it is to move things around, and how motivated the people are to work in industries also matter.

We often hear that a country's rules made by the government can help it grow or make it weaker. When a country is led by experienced, forward-thinking, and selfless leaders, they tend to make rules that help the country grow. But if the leaders are not good, the rules might hurt the country's growth.

It's essential for a nation to pave the way for international manufacturers and become the 'World's Factory.' Initially, these steps might be challenging, requiring the nation to provide various conveniences to foreign companies, from easy setup to commencing operations. Beyond this, offering facilities like automation, labor, power, transportation, supply chain logistics, safety measures, disease control (as seen with COVID-19), peaceful geographical circumstances, and attractive taxation structures contribute to drawing foreign manufacturers in.

Every country should strive to seize this opportunity. Government policies that support such endeavors can position a nation as the next global manufacturing hub.

SUMMARY

"A country should aim to become a global manufacturing hub, and a key component of this goal should be reflected in its budget."

Chapter 15

Black Money – How to Deal with It?

Offer an option to invest in the manufacturing sector only on an ETT (Exempt - Taxable - Taxable) basis. This means exemption from income tax would apply when invested, but the income from the operating activities would be taxable, as well as if such business ceases to exist before a certain period.

Let's talk about the idea of dealing with black money through investing in the manufacturing sector instead of relying on frequent disclosure schemes.

The problem of black money exists almost everywhere. This is money that people haven't paid taxes on, making it illegal. People try to hide it to avoid giving part of it to the government as taxes.

Generally, many countries try to solve this problem by offering programs called "disclosure schemes." These provide opportunities for people to admit they have black money, pay some taxes on it, and then the money becomes legal and need not be hidden. These schemes are often announced to encourage people to come forward and bring concealed money into the GDP of the nation.

But I am of the considered opinion that instead of the above, if a country offers its citizens the opportunity to come forward and invest in new establishments engaged in manufacturing activities, then an amount equal to that investment shall be considered disclosed income. However, other terms and conditions relating to time limits, categories of goods manufactured, the use of indigenous plant and machinery, employment of regional labor, and various other factors may be included and not denied.

What does that mean? It means using hidden money to start or expand (optional) businesses that make things like clothes, gadgets, engineering products, FMCGs, or other items.

In my professional capacity and experience, I see that moving such money from one's locker to a bank perhaps does not leave an equal impact on the country's economy as it would have if people were allowed to invest in new establishments "WITHOUT ANY INQUIRY FROM THE GOVERNMENT'S SIDE." This might be allowed once in a specified period. The greed of saving on income tax, in my opinion, would leave no stone unturned towards the disclosure of such money on the economic graph of that respective country. This would have multi-layered benefits for the government, industry, and people in the future.

Some people may argue for the loss of direct taxes due to the non-disclosure of money. But as the investment in various types of assets would start in the establishment of a new entity, the same or more would come back by way of indirect taxes on the purchase of those assets.

Investing black money in the manufacturing sector would be a good idea instead of just making people confess and pay some taxes. They could use their money to create more jobs and build things that the country needs. This could boost the economy because more products are being made and more people have jobs, which means they'll spend money on other things too.

Think about it like this: If someone has hidden money, they could invest it to build a factory, plant and machinery, other equipment, or office infrastructure, etc., that makes electronic items. This creates jobs for people who work at the factory, people who transport these goods, and people who sell them in stores. The country benefits from more economic activity, increased tax collections, and it becomes a win-win situation.

However, there are challenges too. Ensuring that the money is actually being invested in the right way and that the businesses are operating properly is important. Also, not everyone who has black money might be interested in investing it in manufacturing. They may uproar in many ways and resist the decision of the government. But in the end, they have to be within the ambit of the government's guidelines. If this happens, two further benefits cannot be denied:

1. Hidden money of those who are not directly linked to any business activity has to be invested either by themselves or by someone close to them.
2. Discouragement of corruption as the amenity schemes of the government would have no chance to take place.

SUMMARY

In my opinion, the idea of investing black money in the manufacturing sector instead of relying solely on disclosure schemes has its merits. It could help the country's economy by creating jobs and producing more goods. However, it's important to ensure the investments are genuine and beneficial for the nation as a whole.

Chapter 16

Enhancing Product Utility Through Continuous Innovations

In today's dynamic business landscape, the continuous innovation of products is of utmost importance to ensure the longevity and relevance of a business entity within the market. This practice is not only vital for maintaining market presence but also for promoting business growth. Regularly adding value to products has become increasingly crucial, especially as a substantial portion of the consumer base is now comprised of the younger generation. Young consumers tend to prioritize various features and aspects of products more than their older counterparts, making innovation an essential strategy for capturing their attention and loyalty.

The prevalence of information availability through the Internet has significantly empowered consumers. They can now easily compare features, brands, prices, and after-sales services of various products online before making a purchase decision. This shift in consumer behavior underscores the necessity for businesses to consistently offer innovative products that align with changing preferences and technological advancements.

While traditional buyers might have relied on sellers for guidance, today's consumers are more self-informed and discerning.

As a result, businesses must engage in continuous research and development efforts to introduce novel features, functions, designs, and overall value propositions to their products. This approach enables companies to stay competitive, maintain demand, and secure a loyal customer base.

Industries such as Electronics, Computers, IT, Automotive, building materials, Interior and Exterior Design, and Fashion have exemplified the positive outcomes of integrating innovation into their products. These industries have thrived by embracing technological advancements, novel designs, and continuous improvements in their offerings, effectively meeting consumer demands and expectations.

To provide more understanding of the subject, I quote here some meeting contents of one of the Managing Directors of a Bath Fitting manufacturing company during a Dealers' meet. Here, it was a common thought among all the attendees (Dealers, Distributors, and sales teams) that there is a big recession in the market, making further increases in sales seem impossible as new construction is totally out of the market due to such a big recession. The Managing Director then put an example in the ongoing meeting of a similar trade in Germany where 65% of the total requirements of Bath Fitting are being consumed in the Renovation Market and only 35% is being used in New Construction. This has been possible because new models with the latest features were reaching the market, and people preferred those new products by obsoleting their existing products, which perhaps were also working equally. The latest products were attracting people of that country in high order. In the end, he made his dealers understand that the same position may happen here because the company had already launched a big range of its products with the adoption of the latest technology in its manufacturing process. This has improved its product from all angles, including its appearance, size, new design, better finish, features, and color. Therefore, to capture the renovation market—if the new construction market is depressed for a while—advertise and educate people about the new features and benefits of these innovations.

However, it's imperative to note that there is still room for innovation within the mechanical and engineering sectors. These industries sometimes struggle to keep pace with the rapid innovation seen in sectors like electronics. To remain relevant and competitive, the mechanical and engineering sectors need to increase their efforts in adopting new technologies, automating manual processes, and integrating mechanical automation. While concerns about increased unemployment may arise, the adoption of technology often leads to the creation of new roles and opportunities.

If I recall the period when computers were first introduced in the Indian market, around 1990 to 1995, there was significant concern among professionals in sectors such as accounting, finance, taxation, and design. Many feared that their jobs would be drastically affected. However, as we observed over time, the impact was largely positive, with technology bringing improvements to these fields and creating new opportunities within the profession. Therefore, such fears should be set aside when adopting new technologies in various industry processes. The adoption of technology often leads to expanded roles and new opportunities within industries, rather than merely displacing traditional roles.

Notably, innovation isn't limited to manufacturing industries alone; the service sector equally benefits from continuous advancements. Service industries play a pivotal role in a country's GDP, alongside manufacturing and agriculture.

Embracing innovation in services, such as engineering, architecture, accounting, education, and medical fields, ensures that local professionals remain up-to-date with the latest trends and knowledge, making them preferable over foreign alternatives.

Even within the agricultural sector, innovation plays a transformative role. The adoption of modern techniques for crop preservation, irrigation, and organic farming has elevated the value and quality of agricultural products. Organic produce, for instance, represents a prime example of adding value to products, enhancing their appeal both locally and in the export market.

Exploring cheap alternatives for every costly and limited product well in time is crucial. Delays in research and innovation in these products would diminish the glory of all the efforts made to reach the said goal. Nations that are not disciplined generally make such mistakes and start aggressive actions when the scarcity of that particular product arises in the respective market.

SUMMARY

In conclusion, the continuous evolution of products through innovation is a linchpin for business success and growth. Industries must proactively identify areas for improvement, embrace technological advancements, and create products that resonate with the changing needs and preferences of consumers. The shift towards a circular economy, which emphasizes sustainability and resource optimization, is a progressive model that should be embraced to ensure the long-term viability of businesses and the well-being of our planet.

Innovations across various sectors—such as agriculture, industry, automotive, FMCG, electrical, engineering, and defense—will likely increase demand in both domestic and international markets. Countries that have embraced this approach have often gained a significant share of the international market. Therefore, continuous research and development are essential.

Chapter 17

Optimum Use of Scarce Resources – Natural/Manmade

Every nation has stocks of natural goods as well as produced goods, but they are definitely in limited quantities. As we all know, natural resources cannot be increased by any means. On the contrary, produced resources can be increased, but at a restricted pace and over a period of time. So, those products which are useful for our own purposes as well as for people of other countries should be optimally consumed if we desire to keep the problem at a distance.

This has been well considered from the changing scenario of currency, which we have felt in the last one or two centuries. Presently, the prevailing currency notes are the evolution of gold and silver coins. It has been realized by America that the stock of gold and silver has its limitations regarding the quantitative issuance of currency in the shape of dollars. They also realized that the stock of gold is reducing with the passage of time, along with other benefits also.

It would be worthwhile to mention here that such an exercise should be undertaken before the occurrence of a problem of such shortfalls; otherwise, this would definitely disturb the subsequent systems depending upon it. Seek affordable alternatives to expensive and limited products to make the optimum use of scarce resources. The invention of alternative products with a preference for low costs cannot be denied. It is a continuous process for everyone, which may place us in a comfortable zone when the availability of goods continues and remains at a cheap rate. The stronger the R&D in this regard, which replaces the use of limited and costly stock with abundant and cheap ones, the better it would be. A few countries have left their mark in this area with new innovations and creations, even in existing products. Such innovations have helped those countries capture the global market and earn huge foreign currency along with other benefits like high-level manufacturing, increased employment, increased revenue, and enhanced infrastructure.

Moreover, striving for efficiency in resource utilization aligns closely with sustainable development goals. The concept of the circular economy, which emphasizes reducing waste and recycling materials to extend their utility, aligns perfectly with optimizing the use of finite resources. By finding innovative ways to reduce the consumption of limited resources, nations can significantly contribute to environmental conservation and long-term resource availability.

SUMMARY

In conclusion, the optimal use of both finite natural resources and manufactured goods is not only a strategic imperative but also an ethical commitment to ensuring a stable and thriving global economy. Pursuing cost-effective alternatives through robust research and innovation can lead to sustained economic growth, improved environmental stewardship, and enhanced well-being for both current and future generations.

Chapter 18

Rational Use of Untapped Assets of Public or Religious Institutions

Apart from the resources that are visible to a nation's economic planners, there are certainly other types of assets that generally remain hidden and out of the knowledge of decision-making authorities. Sometimes these assets may be abundant in both quantity and/or value, presenting significant untapped potential.

Formerly, the Governor of the Reserve Bank of India highlighted a staggering fact: approximately 23,000 to 24,000 tons of gold are held within private holdings, religious temples, and similar institutions. The estimated value of this gold could surpass a monumental 1.3 trillion dollars, equivalent to a full year's economic output or the GDP of multiple preceding years (Source: Punjab Kesari dated 2nd December 2021, Business section).

Similarly, another article in the same publication on 25th May 2022 unveiled the economic magnitude of a prominent Indian temple with a staggering economy of 40 billion USD. This realization underscores the necessity for meticulous planning to harness this substantial wealth effectively. By strategically channeling these vast reserves into circulation, there is significant potential to reduce reliance on foreign loans and cut down on interest outflows to other nations.

To actualize this potential, government policies must be strategically designed to empower institutions to contribute their concealed wealth back into the domestic economy. This involves creating an environment where untapped assets can be rationally integrated into the nation's economic fabric.

Notably, the implications of such an approach extend beyond mere economic stimulation. Rationalizing the use of these underutilized assets can contribute to bolstering the nation's financial sovereignty, reducing external debt dependencies, and enhancing its self-reliance.

For this vision to be realized, a multipronged strategy is essential. Collaboration between the public and private sectors, rigorous legal frameworks, and effective monitoring mechanisms are necessary to ensure that the transition of these concealed resources into the mainstream economy is seamless and equitable.

Additionally, while unlocking these latent assets can provide short-term economic relief, it is imperative to also consider their long-term impact on financial stability and national resilience. As these assets are gradually integrated into the economic landscape, the potential to support sectors like education, healthcare, and infrastructure development becomes evident. Such an approach aligns with sustainable development goals and fosters an environment where both present and future generations benefit from the rational use of resources.

SUMMARY

The rational use of dormant resources within public and religious institutions carries profound economic, social, and even ethical implications. Recognizing the immense potential that these concealed assets hold, the implementation of forward-thinking policies can pave the way for substantial economic growth, reduced reliance on foreign loans, and the development of a more robust and self-reliant nation.

Chapter 19

Improving Farming to Support Industry

This chapter explores the important link between farming and industry. Industries need help from farms. Farms give materials to make things in factories. If we can make these materials in our own country, it's better because these materials are more affordable. But if we have to bring them from faraway places, they cost more money. This is because we have to pay extra money at the borders, for carrying them, and for people who make and sell them. So, farms are important for making industries strong.

Making our farms better contributes to a thriving industrial sector. This is because a lot of the things that factories use to create products come from farms. When we enhance our farming practices, it benefits industries by providing them with the necessary raw materials. These raw materials include items like metals, minerals, rubber, cotton, food and chemicals, which are essential for manufacturing various products. Needless to say, the pace of industry cannot run in the next gear without that of the farming sector.

When we produce these raw materials within our own country, they become more affordable. This is important because if we have to import them from other countries, the costs increase due to taxes, transportation fees, and the need for profit. By boosting agriculture and increasing our capacity to produce these materials locally, we can ensure a stable supply for our industries. This not only helps in reducing costs but also strengthens our industrial sector overall.

SUMMARY

To sum up, strengthening agriculture goes hand in hand with developing industries. A robust agricultural sector provides the foundation for a thriving industrial economy by supplying the essential raw materials required for production. This symbiotic relationship between agriculture and industry is vital for the sustainable growth of a nation's economy.

Chapter 20

Agriculture Sector – Contribution to The Nation

The agriculture sector stands as an essential cornerstone of any nation's economy, providing not only sustenance but also contributing significantly to economic growth, employment generation, and overall development. Its multifaceted role encompasses food security, rural livelihoods, export earnings, and environmental sustainability, making it a sector of paramount importance to the well-being and progress of a nation.

Food Availability: The agriculture sector is the primary source of food production, ensuring a steady and reliable supply of food to the nation's population. It plays a critical role in achieving food security by producing crops, livestock, and other agricultural products necessary to meet the dietary needs of the people. A robust agricultural system helps buffer against food price fluctuations and external supply disruptions, safeguarding the nation's ability to feed its citizens.

Employment Generation: Agriculture remains a major employer, especially in developing countries where a substantial portion of the population resides in rural areas. It provides direct and indirect employment opportunities across the value chain, encompassing activities from farming, harvesting, and processing to distribution and marketing. This widespread employment not only reduces unemployment but also alleviates poverty and drives rural development.

Economic Growth and Export Earnings: The agriculture sector contributes significantly to a nation's economic growth by generating revenue through both domestic consumption and export earnings. A well-managed agricultural sector can create a surplus of produce that can be sold on international markets, bringing in foreign exchange and contributing to the country's trade balance. Export-oriented crops, such as cash crops, spices, and fruits, can open up avenues for global trade and enhance the nation's economic resilience.

Rural Development: Agriculture is often synonymous with rural livelihoods. A thriving agricultural sector can transform rural communities by providing opportunities for income generation and improved living standards. Investments in agricultural infrastructure, such as irrigation systems, roads, and storage facilities, can further enhance rural connectivity, enabling farmers to access markets and adopt better agricultural practices.

Environmental Sustainability: Agriculture has a profound impact on the environment, making sustainable agricultural practices crucial. Modern farming methods must balance productivity with environmental preservation. Sustainable practices encompass soil conservation, water management, agroforestry, and organic farming, which minimize negative ecological impacts while ensuring long-term productivity.

Diversification and Innovation: The agriculture sector has evolved beyond traditional crop cultivation to encompass various sub sectors such as horticulture, aquaculture, and agribusiness. Embracing diversification and innovation in these areas can enhance productivity, create new economic opportunities, and improve the sector's resilience to environmental and market changes.

Advancements in Technology: Advances in technology have led to the development of precision agriculture, where data-driven decisions optimize crop yields and resource utilization. Research and innovation in agricultural sciences have resulted in improved seed varieties, disease-resistant crops, and more efficient farming techniques. These technological advancements enhance productivity and sustainability in the sector.

Cultural and Social Significance: Agriculture often carries cultural and historical significance, connecting people to their roots and traditions. Traditional agricultural practices are intertwined with festivals, rituals, and communal celebrations, preserving cultural heritage and fostering social cohesion. These practices help maintain a sense of identity and continuity within communities.

SUMMARY

The agriculture sector's contribution to the nation extends far beyond the production of food. It shapes economies, supports livelihoods, and sustains the environment. Policymakers, farmers, researchers, and communities must work collaboratively to ensure that the agriculture sector continues to thrive, fostering economic development, social progress, and environmental stewardship for the betterment of the nation as a whole.

Chapter 21

Hub of Services

A handful of nations have grasped the importance of the service sector and are eagerly working to establish the necessary infrastructure, essential facilities, and cutting-edge technology. If needed, the education system can be inherently modified so that new generations are trained to prioritize serving their nation first, followed by global contributions. These nations are also focused on preparing their workforce to be highly skilled and capable of serving not only their own country but the entire world. While the service sector's volume is second to manufacturing in terms of contribution, its profit margin ratio often lags behind. However, when examining actual data, the profit-to-earnings ratio in the service sector can sometimes reach an impressive 50% to 70%, surpassing many other sectors.

When a country provides services to the global market, it accelerates the country's exports and positively impacts the global market. An additional benefit is that the demand for services never diminishes; it continues to grow. This is because technology is an ever-evolving process. There is no definitive point where we can declare it as the final stage with no further improvements possible. Can this be said about any field? Absolutely not. In the present scenario, especially with countries actively pursuing digitalization, automation, and computerization, new innovations and improvements are continually occurring across every sector.

Nothing is a final stroke or milestone. Consequently, professionals need to equip themselves to meet new challenges. Need is the mother of Invention, and results emerge from it.

People will always require services, and with technology advancing, there are always new opportunities for innovation. Experts need to continuously learn and adapt to address emerging problems. As mentioned, need is akin to the mother of invention, and positive outcomes arise from it.

SUMMARY

In conclusion, becoming a hub for valuable services is important. Some countries are strengthening their service sectors to make them more effective and beneficial. This not only supports their own economies but also contributes positively to the global economy.

Chapter 22

Enhancing Employment – Opening of Evening Offices

Opening of Evening Offices (through Private Agencies) by Government Departments for Public Convenience

Dear Readers, instead of focusing on the usual topic of citizens expecting increased employment opportunities from their government, I propose a more pragmatic approach. This approach aims to foster employment growth without imposing additional financial burdens on the nation. Assuming the government is already implementing effective revenue-generating policies and cannot increase public expenditure in the short term, we must explore alternative ways to benefit the public.

In Chapter 47, titled 'Control Over Corruption,' I previously discussed the idea of transforming bribes into official facilitation fees as a means to address this social issue. Hence, I have omitted general employment enhancement strategies in this chapter for the sake of conciseness and ease of implementation.

In today's fast-paced world, ensuring public access to government services is crucial for maintaining efficiency and citizen satisfaction.

One innovative solution to address this issue is the establishment of evening offices by government departments, in collaboration with private agencies. These evening offices would operate during non-traditional hours, providing citizens with the flexibility to access government services outside of their regular work hours.

To outline the functioning and advantages, evening offices would operate during extended hours beyond the standard 9-to-5 schedule. These offices would cater to citizens who find it challenging to take time off from their jobs or businesses during regular working hours to handle government-related tasks. In a nutshell, these private offices would act as an intermediary between government offices and the public, offering flexibility in time.

The required guidelines for the operation of these private evening offices should be established to ensure smooth and risk-free functioning. Efforts should be made to encompass a wide range of government departments, including but not limited to tax collection, permit applications, licensing, and more. Citizens may have the option to schedule appointments or utilize online platforms for specific services, streamlining the process and reducing wait times.

The implementation of evening offices would offer several benefits, including reduced congestion by spreading out the demand for government services over extended hours, thereby mitigating long wait times during regular working hours. Increasing the accessibility of government services would allow citizens with busy daytime commitments to engage with their government seamlessly.

This proposal would also generate employment opportunities in various sectors within the private sector. Additionally, recruitment in other sectors such as administrative staff, security personnel, and support services could contribute to job creation if the government has the capacity to employ them in the operation of these evening offices.

At the same time, we should not ignore that while evening offices can bring about substantial advantages, potential disadvantages should also be considered, particularly the increased operating costs. Security concerns may be another issue for these government departments. Adequate security measures must be in place to ensure the safety of citizens, government employees, and agency holders. Additionally, the coordination of staff schedules and ensuring that the necessary services are available during evening hours may pose logistical challenges.

SUMMARY

In conclusion, the establishment of evening offices by government departments can significantly enhance public convenience by providing more flexible access to essential services. The advantages, such as increased accessibility, reduced congestion, and employment opportunities, can outweigh the disadvantages with careful planning and implementation. To ensure a smooth transition, a well-thought-out strategy and stakeholder engagement are essential. This initiative not only modernizes government service delivery but also aligns with the evolving needs of the workforce and the public.

Chapter 23

Digitalization

In the 21st century, the transformative power of digitalization has been reshaping societies across the globe, and its impact on nation-building is undeniable. Digitalization, which encompasses the adoption of digital technologies and the integration of data-driven processes into various aspects of a nation's functioning, plays a pivotal role in shaping the economic, social, and political landscape of a country. This essay explores the multifaceted role of digitalization in nation-building, shedding light on its implications for economic growth, governance, education, and social inclusivity.

Economic Growth and Innovation

Digitalization is a potent driver of economic growth and innovation. When a nation embraces digital technologies, it empowers businesses to streamline operations, reduce costs, and reach new markets. E-commerce platforms, for example, have enabled even small and medium-sized enterprises to access a global customer base. Additionally, digital innovation hubs and startups flourish in a digitalized environment, fostering entrepreneurship and job creation.

Moreover, digitalization fuels research and development, leading to breakthroughs in various sectors such as healthcare, renewable energy, and artificial intelligence. This, in turn, enhances a nation's competitiveness on the global stage, attracting foreign investment and bolstering economic resilience.

Effective Governance and Public Services

Efficient governance is a cornerstone of nation-building, and digitalization can significantly enhance the effectiveness of public administration. Digital tools enable governments to streamline bureaucratic processes, reduce corruption, and improve transparency. E-governance initiatives facilitate citizen engagement by providing online platforms for services, consultations, and feedback.

Furthermore, data analytics and artificial intelligence enable governments to make informed decisions based on real-time data, enhancing policy formulation and implementation. Digitalization also enhances public safety and security through advanced surveillance and emergency response systems.

Education and Skill Development

Digitalization revolutionizes education by making knowledge accessible to a wider audience. Online learning platforms and digital resources facilitate lifelong learning, skill development, and vocational training. This not only empowers individuals but also strengthens the workforce, making a nation more competitive in the global economy.

Digital education also bridges the urban-rural education gap, ensuring that remote and marginalized communities have access to quality educational resources. In the long run, a well-educated and skilled populace contributes to a nation's human capital and economic prosperity.

Social Inclusivity and Connectivity

Digitalization can promote social inclusivity by connecting remote and marginalized communities to the digital world. Access to the internet and digital devices empowers individuals with information, access to services, and opportunities for economic participation. Social networks and online communities foster social cohesion and provide a platform for civic engagement.

Moreover, telemedicine and remote healthcare services improve healthcare access in rural areas, reducing health disparities. Digitalization also supports disaster preparedness and response, enhancing a nation's resilience in the face of natural disasters and crises.

SUMMARY

The role of digitalization in the building of a nation cannot be overstated. It transforms economies, enhances governance, promotes education, and fosters social inclusivity. As nations continue to embrace digital technologies, they must also address the challenges of digital divides, data privacy, and cybersecurity to ensure that the benefits of digitalization are accessible to all citizens. By harnessing the full potential of digitalization, nations can embark on a path of sustainable development, prosperity, and inclusive growth, ultimately shaping a brighter future for their citizens.

Chapter 24
Green Development

This refers to progress in any field without affecting or compromising the natural, social, or other elements, in the interest of both citizens and the nation.

Green Development: Nurturing a Sustainable Nation

Introduction

In an era marked by environmental challenges, the concept of green development has emerged as a powerful framework for building nations that prioritize not only economic progress but also the well-being of their citizens and the preservation of natural and social ecosystems. Green development, often referred to as sustainable development, is a holistic approach that seeks to foster progress in various fields without compromising the delicate balance of nature and the social fabric of society. This essay explores the multifaceted role of green development in the nation-building process and its implications for the environment, society, and long-term prosperity.

Environmental Sustainability

At the heart of green development lies the commitment to safeguarding the environment. Nations embracing green development strategies prioritize renewable energy sources, reduce carbon emissions, and enhance resource efficiency. They enact policies and regulations that promote the conservation of natural resources, protection of biodiversity, and sustainable land use practices.

Investments in green technologies and eco-friendly infrastructure not only reduce environmental harm but also create green jobs and drive economic growth. By taking proactive steps to mitigate climate change and minimize pollution, nations ensure a healthier and more resilient environment for current and future generations.

Social Inclusivity and Equity

Green development places a strong emphasis on social inclusivity and equity. It seeks to uplift marginalized communities and ensure that the benefits of progress are distributed equitably. This includes providing access to education, healthcare, and economic opportunities for all citizens.

Furthermore, green development encourages community participation in decision-making processes, especially in projects that affect local environments. By involving citizens, particularly those most impacted by development initiatives, nations can ensure that development projects are culturally sensitive and socially sustainable.

Economic Resilience and Innovation

Contrary to the notion that green development hinders economic growth; it can actually enhance a nation's economic resilience and foster innovation. Investments in clean energy, sustainable agriculture, and green technologies lead to the creation of new industries and job opportunities.

Moreover, green development encourages resource-efficient practices that reduce production costs and increase competitiveness. Nations that prioritize green development often find themselves at the forefront of innovation, exporting sustainable solutions to global markets.

Long-term Vision and Global Leadership

Green development is not just about short-term gains; it's about crafting a vision for the long-term well-being of a nation. Nations that champion green development set an example on the global stage by demonstrating environmental responsibility and ethical governance.

They engage in international collaborations to address global challenges, such as climate change and biodiversity loss, while advocating for sustainable practices and environmental protection. This not only elevates their international standing but also strengthens diplomatic ties and cooperation.

SUMMARY

Green development is a visionary approach to nation-building that recognizes the interconnectedness of economic, social, and environmental well-being. It is a blueprint for fostering progress that leaves no one behind while ensuring that the natural world is preserved for future generations. As nations strive for development, they must embrace green principles, innovate sustainably, and balance economic growth with ecological and social responsibility. In doing so, they will create a legacy of prosperity, equity, and environmental stewardship that stands the test of time.

Chapter 25

Restricting Inflation

A little bit of inflation, around 1-3%, can actually help a country's economy grow better. The mood of the market remains cheerful, both psychologically and due to an increase in demand from various sectors. A good example is the demand for equity shares or mutual funds in respective stock exchanges during periods of rising share price indices.

Several times, we notice that the prices of things like food, clothes, and other items are going up just a little bit each year – maybe around 2-3%. This is what we call inflation. It might sound like a bad thing, but a small amount of inflation can actually be helpful for a country's economy.

Here's why:

When there's a small, predictable amount of inflation, it can encourage people to spend and invest their money. If they know that prices will go up a bit, they might be more likely to buy things now rather than waiting, which can help businesses sell their products and services. This, in turn, can lead to more jobs being created because businesses need more people to help meet the demand.

When people spend more money and businesses are doing well, the overall economy tends to grow. This means that the country is producing more goods and services, and people are earning more money. It's like a cycle – spending and investing creates more economic activity, which leads to more jobs and even more spending.

Additionally, a little bit of inflation can make it easier for people who owe money, like loans or mortgages. If prices are going up a bit, wages and salaries usually rise too. This means that even if you owe money, you might be earning more, making it a bit easier to pay back what you owe.

On the contrary, deflation might sound appealing because prices are going down, but it can actually cause problems. When prices keep dropping, people might wait to buy things because they think they'll get even cheaper later. This can slow down businesses and lead to fewer jobs. Additionally, if you owe money, like a loan, it becomes harder to pay back because the money you owe is worth more.

So, which one is better? Most experts think a little bit of inflation is better than deflation. Too much inflation is not good, but a small amount can help the economy grow. Deflation, on the other hand, can make things tricky and slow down economic activity.

Think of it like this: balance is important. Just like how a little bit of rain is good for plants, a little bit of inflation is good for the economy. But just like too much rain can cause floods, too much inflation or deflation can cause economic problems.

In the end, both inflation and deflation have their pros and cons, but a gentle, controlled amount of inflation is usually considered better for a country's economy. Too much inflation is not good either. If prices rise too quickly and unpredictably, it can make it hard for people to plan their spending and it can erode the value of their savings. So, it's like finding a balance – a small, controlled amount of inflation can help an economy grow, but it's important not to let it get out of control.

SUMMARY

We must have seen that industries flourish only in the case of an inflationary trend. A little bit of inflation, around 2-3%, can actually be good for a country's economy. It encourages people to spend and invest, helps businesses grow, and creates more jobs. Just like seasoning in food, a touch of inflation can add flavor to the economy and keep things moving smoothly.

(B) IMPORT/EXPORT POLICIES

Chapter 26

Export Policies: Exports of Goods & Services – At Affordable Prices

Boosting a country's exports is always a positive sign. When those exports are competitively priced compared to other exporting nations, it becomes easier to capture the international market. However, this shouldn't come at the expense of compromising the quality of goods or services. Sacrificing quality for the sake of cheap exports can create significant issues for exporting nations and may even lead to a loss of reputation in importing countries. It's important to note that once the impression of poor quality or service spreads in the import market, regaining the earlier position becomes a harder task than starting from scratch.

Initially, an importer's first consideration is the availability and price of the products they want to import. However, over time, quality becomes increasingly important. It becomes the key factor that allows an exporter to maintain their presence in the import market. Establishing trust in the quality of products within the importing country is vital. Gradually increasing prices after gaining consumer confidence is recommended. At the initial stages, prioritizing higher profits should be set aside in such transactions.

Chapter 27

Motivating Exports Through Modern Techniques

Let's find ways to increase a country's exports even more, building on the improvements that have already been made.

Using new ways of doing things in different fields helps businesses get more customers. In recent years, technology has changed a lot in industries like engineering, automobiles, electricity, machines, and even farming and services. Long ago, nobody thought farming would change so much. People believed farming was just about watering crops and taking care of them until they were ready to harvest. But now, things have changed. Farming has become really advanced with things like better irrigation, safe crops, and the use of good seeds and fertilizers. There's even a type of farming called organic farming that makes healthy food. This has not only made food better but also increased its value. Other fields have also grown a lot with new inventions becoming real.

For businesses to do well in today's world, they need to use new technology quickly. This makes sure they can still do well compared to others. It's like when we first went to space or used remote controls for devices from far away.

We can see that businesses that keep using new ideas are growing. So, everyone should try to use the latest technology in what they do.

This way, they can compete with products from their country and other countries. People now know a lot about products, so it's important to use good technology to make things that people will like. Waiting too long to try new things might make people not like what's being made, even if it took a lot of work to make it. So, whether someone makes things or provides services, they should keep up with new technology. This helps them stay strong in a competitive market.

Many times, I have seen that the adoption of the latest technology saves our cost of running & cost production of material also. We are all aware that the level of production is increasing year after year. This could only be possible because of the adoption of new technology. If demand is there, establish your plant with new machines although the existing one is good the level of production is lacking. In such a situation forecast the volume of demand that would persist in the period ahead and if our cost of changes in new techniques gets recovered from an increased level of production in a reasonable period, these changes are recommendable.

At the same time, compromising on quality should not be entirely ignored, as it may lead to the negative effects associated with a 'short-term approach' for the business. Therefore, adopting a balanced approach is always preferable. Do continue to walk on this pattern and gain benefits to the maximum extent. However, the adoption of new technology has a major strategic impact. Consequently, it has been recognized that an effective planning system should be there to capitalize on the opportunities offered by such technologies.

SUMMARY

Using new techniques, innovations in new Designs, Quality, after-sale service and other Features etc., is always preferable to attract customers. This has been seen that a product with a new design or features creates the demand even from that market where it was thought that no more requirement was required or the market was already filled. The reason behind this is that people love to change their products if they find new things with more features, size, shape etc. in the market in spite of the fact that they already have the same thing but with some old comforts & utilities.

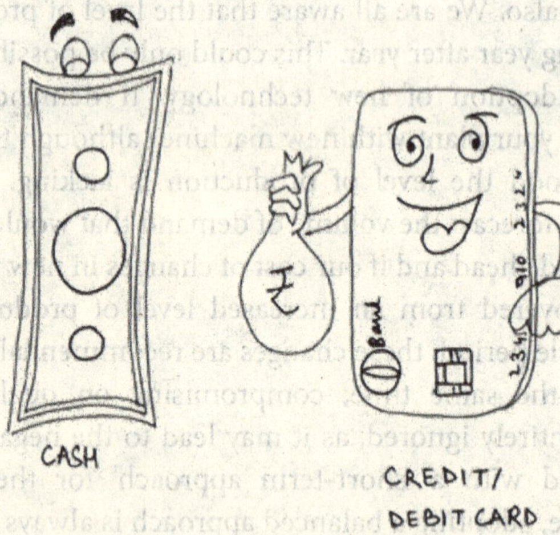

Chapter 28

Exporting Services for National Growth

There's a new opportunity for a country to make more money by selling services to other nations. People who are good at their jobs, like experts and those who are pretty good, can help by providing services to other countries that aren't as good at the latest technology. Just like making things, the government needs to make really good schools, places for technology businesses, advanced space and defense technology, special knowledge about cars, and other machines, farming, and more things like that. Countries that are really good at these things can be better off than others, both with money and having a big influence. It's important to focus on sending out both the knowledge and the things made from it because this would help a lot of big, medium, and small businesses to grow and give many people jobs. But, we shouldn't forget about providing services too.

When we talk about selling services to other countries, we should also think about the people from our country who go to work in other places. The government should help them so that they can work easily and do well. This would encourage other people from our country to go to other countries, work, and make money too.

Exporting services is like sharing our skills and expertise

with other countries, which can help our country's economy grow even stronger. When we send our skilled professionals to other nations, we're not just helping them, but also building a positive image for our country on the global stage.

Imagine a world where our universities, technology hubs, and research centers become so advanced that people from all around the world want to learn from us. This would not only bring in money through education and research collaborations but also create a reputation for excellence.

Moreover, when we export services, we're not just selling knowledge; we're creating connections and collaborations that can lead to groundbreaking discoveries and innovations. By sharing our know-how with others, we're contributing to the advancement of various fields on an international level.

SUMMARY

So, while we focus on selling physical goods, let's not forget the immense potential of exporting our skills, ideas, and solutions. This two-pronged approach can truly catapult our country's development and position us as a leader in the global arena.

Chapter 29

Exploring New Markets

Every product has a huge market, maybe even endless in some cases. To make our business bigger, we need to keep looking for new places to sell our things. I've traveled across almost 70-80% of India and many foreign countries and I've noticed that some things sold in one place are not found in another. Usually, I visit each place at least twice before deciding. Sometimes, our sales team has extra time to explore new markets without neglecting their current ones. They can work from a distance through the internet or phones to connect with existing or potential customers. Instead of spending more money on new staff, we can give this task to our current team. When our product orders increase, it encourages us to work harder and adjust our production to meet the demand. This lowers the cost of making each item and boosts the organization's profits.

Finding new markets is important because we can't be sure that our business will keep growing forever. Things are changing all the time - in technology, science, and business. This makes our products have a short life in the market.

If a business does this in other countries, not just its own, it can help its own growth and the economies of the countries where it operates. More money from other countries will come in, which will help our country grow. This also leaves space in the local market for smaller businesses that can't go to foreign markets. This approach demonstrates care for the nation and its people by allowing them to benefit from the local market.

Remember, when entering new markets, some adjustments to our product might be necessary. People in different regions might have varying preferences, desire more or fewer features, or require specific adaptations. It's beneficial to tailor our product to meet the needs and wants of the local customer base. Additionally, incorporating new and appealing designs can further enhance the product's fit within the new market. Therefore, strive to make your product compatible with the requirements of customers in those areas, incorporating new and attractive designs, so that relevant products can establish their place in the new market.

SUMMARY

To sum up, don't assume that our current customers are all we need. Look for new markets where people might want our products, or where we can create that desire with some extra effort. When exploring new markets, especially in other countries, we should ensure that our products align with the tastes and needs of those consumers. This approach benefits both our business and our nation's growth.

Chapter 30

Foreign Currency Reserves

While increasing exports automatically leads to an accumulation of foreign currency, our efforts shouldn't end there. We should strive to maximize these earnings. Maintaining a surplus of foreign currency offers numerous advantages and contributes to building national resilience, while also helping to maintain the value of our own currency.

The majority of foreign currency comes from selling goods and services to other countries. However, additional strategies can further bolster these reserves:

Attracting Tourism: Let's work on making our country an attractive destination for international visitors. We can develop our unique sites into tourist attractions that can be utilized for various events, business meetings, international political gatherings, media productions, and even filming locations for foreign film industries. By providing excellent facilities and potentially even offering subsidies, we can entice more visitors to come and spend their money here.

Global Trade Hub: We can elevate our country's position to become a key player in global trade. By establishing a favorable environment for international companies to conduct business here, and by implementing minimal taxes on international transactions, we can stimulate a greater flow of foreign currency into the nation.

Encourage Investments by Expats: Motivating citizens who work abroad to invest their savings back home can be quite beneficial. This not only strengthens our financial foundations but also bolsters our foreign currency reserves.

Boost Remittances: Encouraging expatriates working in foreign countries to send their earnings back to their homeland can lead to a twofold advantage. First, our nation's financial stability improves, and second, our foreign currency reserves expand.

In addition to these initiatives, regular research and innovation play a crucial role. We should proactively seek out cost-effective alternatives for expensive and scarce products. Rather than waiting for shortages to arise, we should be preemptive in finding substitutes and improving our self-reliance.

SUMMARY

Accumulating a healthy stock of foreign currency is pivotal. It equips us to face uncertainties and ensures the strength of our nation's currency. Let's persist in discovering innovative methods to increase our foreign currency reserves, thereby fortifying our country's position on the global stage and fostering economic stability.

Chapter 31

Reducing Imports

We can make our country's industries stronger by buying less stuff from other countries. To stop things from coming in that hurt our own businesses, jobs, and services, we can make some rules. These rules can range from controlling the amount of money we spend on foreign things to even stopping them completely. We can also make foreign stuff more expensive by adding a tax when they come into our country.

Countries that are still growing often face a problem where they spend more money on buying things from other places than they earn by selling their own things. This is called a "Trade Deficit." Things like oil, gas, gold, materials for making things, food, and even medicines are examples of things we buy from other countries, and we need to control how much we buy.

One good way to reduce how much we need to buy from other places is to start making more things ourselves. This means we need places where we study and invent new ideas, and also learn how to make things. However small and medium businesses might need help from the government to do this because it's not easy for them to do it all on their own.

People like you and me can also help by not using things that we can't make in our own country. If we can, we should avoid using things that we have to buy from other places.

When we reduce our dependence on purchasing from other countries, we not only help our own industries grow but also make our country more self-reliant. This means we can stand on our own feet and be less dependent on others.

Imagine if we had more factories and workshops where we produced goods ourselves. This would create more jobs for our people and boost our economy, effectively building a stronger foundation for our country.

And by supporting local businesses and the products they create; we can cultivate a sense of pride and unity within our country. When we choose to buy things made by our own people, we're essentially investing in the future of our nation. It's a powerful statement that demonstrates our belief in our own capabilities.

SUMMARY

Making Our Country Strong by Reducing Reliance on Imports.

Chapter 32

Importing Raw Materials Instead of Finished Goods

Another milestone we can achieve by continuing on this path is prioritizing the import of raw materials over finished goods. This shift can bring several advantages to a country's economy and industries. Raw materials are the fundamental building blocks that industries utilize to create finished products. When a country opts to import raw materials and then process them domestically, it sets the stage for more robust and sustainable economic growth.

One key advantage lies in the fact that importing raw materials allows a country to add value to its own economy through the manufacturing process. By producing finished goods locally, a nation can create more jobs, enhance the development of valuable skills within its workforce, and generate higher revenues. This approach fosters the growth of local industries, which in turn contributes to economic stability and a greater degree of self-sufficiency.

Another advantage is that importing raw materials provides flexibility and customization. When a country imports finished goods, it may have limited control over the product's quality, design, and specifications. In contrast, importing raw materials allows domestic industries to tailor the manufacturing process to meet specific demands, resulting in products that better suit local preferences and market trends.

Furthermore, relying on raw material imports can foster a culture of innovation within industries. The need to efficiently process and transform these raw materials into high-quality finished products compels industries to develop advanced manufacturing techniques and technologies. This drive for innovation can lead to the creation of new technologies, patents, and intellectual property that hold value not only domestically but also in global markets.

Importing raw materials often translates to a reduction in transportation costs. Finished goods, by their very nature, are bulkier and require more space for shipping, which inflates transportation expenses. Conversely, raw materials can be more compact and lightweight, leading to a decrease in both shipping costs and the environmental impact associated with transportation.

Last but not least, importing raw materials can pave the way for stronger international trade relationships. Countries exporting raw materials benefit from the demand generated by importing nations. This reciprocal exchange can foster mutually beneficial trade agreements and partnerships, ultimately enhancing diplomatic and economic ties.

SUMMARY

Importing raw materials offers a pathway to economic growth, job creation, customization, innovation, cost efficiency, and stronger international relationships. By nurturing local industries and adding value through the manufacturing process, a country can strategically position itself for long-term prosperity and competitiveness in the global market.

(C) INCREASE IN REVENUE

Chapter 33

Optimal Use of Idle Assets: Moveable Property

When we have things that are not being used, like old equipment or other items the government owns, we can make smart choices to benefit our nation. Here's why it's a good idea:

Saves Money in Maintenance: Unused assets still cost money to maintain. By selling or disposing of these things, we can stop spending money on them.

Makes Money by Disposing of Unused Assets: We can sell these unused items and generate revenue. This money can then be used for important things like helping the public, paying off loans to save on interest, or investing in projects that bring in more money for the country.

Meeting Departmental Needs Through Redeployment: Sometimes, one government department may have surplus assets that another department can utilize. This facilitates efficient resource allocation, ensuring these items are used where they're most needed.

Maintaining Essential Stock Levels: Government departments should only hold onto assets that they can actively use. If an item is no longer useful, a well-defined plan for its disposition should be implemented.

Maximizing Resource Utilization: Idle valuable assets benefit no one. By ensuring wise use of our resources, we can build a stronger and more efficient nation.

Chapter 34

Optimal Use of Idle Assets: Immovable Property

We can achieve significant benefits for our nation by making optimal use of the land and buildings we already possess. Here are two key strategies:

Government-Owned Land: When the government has vacant land or buildings, it can develop them and then lease them out to individuals or businesses. For instance, if there's an empty space, the government could construct facilities like storage sheds, parking lots, or warehouses on it and then allow others to utilize them. This approach generates revenue for the government while also maximizing the value of the land.

Welcoming Foreign Investment: We can also invite individuals from other countries to invest in these projects. Their involvement can aid us in developing the land or buildings, which can create employment opportunities and bring additional revenue into our nation. By implementing these strategies, we can ensure that the land and buildings we have are not wasted, and instead contribute to a stronger and more prosperous country.

Chapter 35

Unlocking Potential in Natural Resources

Discovering and Utilizing Our Natural Treasures for a Stronger Nation

We can take a significant step towards national improvement by finding and utilizing the valuable resources native to our land and environment.

Here's how it benefits us:

Finding More Resources: We should search for more valuable resources in our country, such as minerals, oil, or unique plants. When we find them, we should use them wisely. Regular research and engineering efforts are needed to explore such resources, guided by competent leadership.

Using Them Wisely: We can use these valuable resources in two ways. Some can be sold to other countries to generate revenue (this is called exporting), while others can be used domestically to produce goods or meet our own needs. By finding and utilizing our natural resources wisely, we can strengthen and enrich our nation, create jobs, and build things right here at home.

Chapter 36

Development Of Tourism

Different countries around the world have realized how important tourism is for their growth. However, how much they focus on tourism can vary from country to country, depending on their government's approach. Many factors influence this, like the country's size, natural beauty, laws, weather, safety, transportation, and infrastructure. Even how local people feel about tourism can make a big difference.

Some countries rely on tourism to make money. When people from all over the world visit, the country can earn foreign money. So, the big question is, how can a country attract both foreign tourists and its citizens to visit? This is something the local government, state government, or national government needs to figure out. They need to offer things like entertainment options and follow the laws to make it attractive for visitors. Kinds of sources of entertainment are highly recommendable with the broader approach as per the law. If the current laws are too strict, they might need to change them to make their country more appealing than others.

In recent years, the film industry has played a big part in the service sector's growth. It's important to welcome people from the film industry and give them incentives like tax breaks to encourage them to work in your country. At the same time, it's a good idea to make sure your own country's film industry stays active at home instead of going abroad. Otherwise, efforts towards the first mentioned would lose its glory & respective benefits. This can help your nation's economy and reputation grow.

Chapter 37

Tax Policies: Favoring More Money in People's Pockets

Every country has a plan for spending and saving money, called a budget. Without going into much detail about the logic behind such a setup, a government's operations are shaped by its budgetary plans. The effectiveness of such a plan is paramount to the nation's well-being. Before explaining the main part of this topic, let's acknowledge that priorities are constantly changing. Over longer periods, income and expenditure priorities cannot remain static. This is because there are numerous areas requiring government support to uplift various sectors, such as industrial growth, agriculture, socio-economic development, infrastructure development, and public benefits delivered through the tax system.

When it comes to deciding how to tax people, whether through direct taxes (like income tax) or indirect taxes (like sales tax), it's crucial to consider the amount of money people have left over as "disposable income" after tax payments. When people have sufficient disposable income, they are more likely to spend it in the market. This increased spending generates demand for products, which in turn leads to higher industrial production, increased employment opportunities, and ultimately, higher government revenue from the sale of these goods. This cycle then repeats, with the government's earnings derived from these sales contributing back to the government's exchequer.

Here, a practice has been observed where many times a particular government, although maintaining the same tax structure, utilizes different modus operandi. They take the opposing route of minimizing taxes by creating a shortage of money in the hands of the public. This can be a major mistake because it makes money scarce in the economy, leading to slowed or halted growth. This is clearly undesirable.

The second benefit is also quite significant in terms of maintaining the upper level of the tax structure. A reverse situation occurs: to save tax out of their earned income, people can transfer their income to any of the investment segments set up by the government. The reason may be to collect money from people through specific investments that the government can then utilize for national needs. In this scenario, people are compelled to outflow their money into such schemes for tax savings. Here, the respective government could collect tax only once from the people and also use their savings for national needs.

On the other hand, if tax rates are reduced on high income brackets while disregarding investment policies, the government can still collect tax through the sale of products to these people. There are also other benefits associated with this approach.

The third benefit, as seen in many countries, involves a much simpler tax structure that eliminates the need to claim deductions after investments. Are there other compliance parameters for availing tax deductions?

One potential opposition to this proposal that comes to mind is that it might demotivate savings meant for future social security due to the absence of tax incentives for saving.

However, people invest for reasons beyond tax benefits. Here are two other key reasons:

1. To secure themselves against the costs of medical treatment.
2. To secure themselves financially in case they experience a loss of income.

For the first reason, regarding the need for security against medical expenses, periodic investments are essential in most countries. As the designated period elapses, the benefits become unavailable. However, securing oneself for a longer period by initially investing in a scheme may not be an option in the future. Even if such schemes are available, the uncertainty of health and the tedious terms and conditions might make them undesirable.

The second reason is highly sensitive. Special attention should be paid to covering the risk of those who feel they may not have future earnings to meet basic living expenses. For this reason alone, a PENSION SCHEME with tax benefits is essential. Tax benefits for all other types of savings' schemes could be reduced to zero, with a possible upper limit being established. Considering the specific needs of non-working women, offering additional tax benefits to male members of their families wouldn't be unreasonable. Furthermore, promoting financial literacy programs can empower individuals to make informed investment decisions for their future.

Regarding a nation's wealth availability, I believe it's not a new concept for any country. In this era, most countries must have already achieved their targeted economic positions.

(D) REDUCTION IN EXPENSES

Chapter 38

Defense Sector Expenses

Defense Sector Spending and Building a Nation

With the cooperation of all the countries in the world, achievement in this area can be gained. We all know that a huge amount of a country's budget is being allocated to buy defense equipment for the armed forces, safety measures on international borders, and so on. Whereas allocation of such budget expenses gets reduced in other areas like social welfare, the economic sector, other progressive fronts, etc. This happens because every country, even if it's the richest as compared to the others, has a certain limit when it comes to allocating overall expenditure budget.

I don't think we should completely get rid of defense spending, but we can reduce it. Even if we have peaceful relations with our neighbors, we still need some defense forces, equipment, and border security to avoid conflicts and protect our country in our geographical area. Because the armed forces and expenses on the other side are not only meant for defending a country from the outside's powers but are also supposed to keep peace within the country, fight against natural calamities, provide security in matters that are not routine, say the period of elections, celebration of national events or festivals, and last but not least, a fear in the mind of the culprits causing harm to the nation.

Defense spending is not just for defending against outside threats; it also helps maintain peace within our borders, respond to natural disasters, and ensure safety during special events like elections or national celebrations.

To build a strong nation, we should focus on making things within our country instead of relying too much on imports, especially for defense equipment and natural resources. Now, something I'm thinking about (though I'm not an expert or an officer of the Central Bank) is that if needed, we could consider printing extra money to pay for defense expenses, as long as it doesn't make prices go up too much (inflation). This might go against some international rules, say the International Monetary Fund (IMF) or Central Bank policies, but it could be good for your country if done carefully.

If we look at how much different countries spend on defense over time, we'll see that if we didn't have to spend so much on defense, we could use that money for other important things that benefit our people and our nation.

Chapter 39

One Country – One Election

Streamlining Elections for a Stronger Nation

Yes, I do not know what the opinions would be of those individuals or political parties that are directly or indirectly providing materials or other services during election periods. They might have concerns because their livelihoods depend on elections. Similarly, political parties may have varying opinions on holding simultaneous elections at the central, state, or local levels. In a country with many states, different factions within a single party may have differing views on the timing of elections. Some parties might prefer staggered election times in different states for their own benefit.

However, if we set aside these concerns and focus on the potential benefits, they could be significant. First, it could save a lot of money because we wouldn't have to conduct elections so frequently. During election time, government work often slows down, and important decisions get delayed because of election rules. Even if some urgent work needs to be done, it often ends up being influenced by election campaigns, which isn't always fair.

The growth-oriented proposals have also been stalled due to the application of Election Codes, absences from offices by the ruling party, and similar factors. Even minimal work during this period tends to be influenced by the election campaign, either directly or indirectly, often in a way that benefits certain segments of society. The private sector is also indirectly affected by frequent elections held with short intervals. An individual might not recognize that they managed to handle their work during this period, but collectively, they experienced difficulties due to these challenges. If these frequent elections were spaced out over a period of, say, four or five years, the resulting output would likely be more positive.

Another major benefit of having a single election is the reduction in expenditure associated with multiple elections, which the government incurs whenever they occur. Rather than focusing solely on the optimal use of these expenditures, I would emphasize the need to consolidate elections into a single event across the entire country.

A significant portion of these expenses, such as those for petroleum products and digital marketing, often flows out of the country in foreign exchange. The remaining expenses incurred domestically may be argued to generate revenue for some, but they do not significantly impact the country's GDP.

Furthermore, these expenses are not considered Capital Expenditure (Capex), which would create an asset. Instead, they disappear once the election is over. Holding elections less frequently could save a substantial amount of money for the country.

Many experts have already suggested this system as a way to save government money. It's a matter that all political parties in parliament should seriously consider.

A serious consideration of this is thought is deeply required by all the parties in Parliament with common consent.

Additionally, holding a single election for multiple levels

of government would make voters more deliberate when casting their votes. They would need to choose candidates for the central government, state government, and local government all at once. This approach would encourage voters to consider the capabilities of individual candidates rather than simply voting for a single party that might be experiencing an election wave or 'Lahar' in its favor. Voters might select one candidate from one party for the central government and another capable candidate from a different party for the state government, and so on.

It is commonly believed that this method would ensure that the worth of each candidate would remain in the mind of the public while casting their valuable votes. The likelihood of knowledgeable candidates emerging would be higher, as we often observe shifts in favor of different parties in various elections. Voters would then have to decide whether to follow a party's swing across all elections or to make separate decisions for each election based on different parties.

In this system, voters would have more power, and the choice of who wins would depend on the people. Of course, there could be criticisms that the central ruling party might benefit more in all the elections, but ultimately, it would encourage voters to vote based on the capabilities of the candidates rather than just party loyalty.

Vote for candidates' abilities, not just their party.

Although the approach of a party has its place to decide for the voters to whom to vote or to whom not, still, the capabilities of the candidate should equally weigh who can rightfully keep the public voice in the ruling government.

So, while political parties have their role in guiding voters, it's equally important to consider the qualifications of individual candidates who can effectively represent the public's voice in the government. This doesn't mean that the same party has to be preferred in all types of elections; voters can choose candidates from different parties based on their capabilities. A question may arise in several minds: if a junior candidate is quite competent and senior leaders of the party are not, then how would he be able to do his best for society despite his limitations? I accept this argument to some extent and believe that in matters where senior party leaders are involved, there might be limitations. However, in matters where he is independent and can act within his jurisdiction, he may carry out his duties according to his wishes.

It is rightly said, *"We cannot conceal the rays of light forever. Sooner or later, they will shine."*

In the end, a system where all elections occur simultaneously could empower the people more and encourage them to make informed choices, leading to a stronger and more responsive government.

Elections and Their Campaigning

Elections and Winning Strategies for a Strong Nation

As we are talking about elections, good governance is always deemed to make a country prosperous, self-dependent, powerful, and aggressive in all-round development. But sometimes we see that a political party, despite good governance, still loses the next elections to the opposition parties. Such a situation arises due to a number of visible or invisible reasons that take place during the election period. Out of the abundance of reasons, some are written with an unbiased approach so that any political party promoting good governance may not lose from winning:

(a) **Avoid Overconfidence and Arrogance:** Approach every election as a fresh challenge, regardless of how many elections the party has won in the past from the same constituency. Nothing should be taken for granted. Continuous winning can lead to complacency, less innovation in public welfare work, and fewer new ideas.

(b) **Provide Welfare Schemes:** If other parties are announcing benefits for the people, the discussed party should not lag behind. Failing to do so might result in unfavorable outcomes, as everyone desires a better lifestyle. Even a small saving in their regular expenses can influence their voting preferences, just as people deposit their money in banks that offer higher interest rates within safety limits.

(c) **Explain Your Mistakes in a Way That Highlights Indirect Benefits to the Public.**

(d) **Maintain Politeness in Dressing and Body Language:** After winning one or two elections, candidates sometimes change their public image to reflect an arrogant attitude. Voters lose interest when they perceive arrogance, so candidates should avoid this.

(e) **Present the entire party as competent:** No single person can advance the party alone. Showcase all department leaders as fully capable to ensure people understand that the party's effectiveness relies on the collective strength of its leadership, not just a few individuals

(f) **Avoid Constantly Criticizing Other Parties:** Repeatedly pointing out the shortcomings of other parties doesn't leave a good impression on the public. It spreads negativity and discourages others from listening to you.

(g) **Occasionally acknowledge the good actions of the opposition:** If the opposition has made positive contributions to the nation or offers valuable suggestions, recognizing this demonstrates open-mindedness and can win public favor.

Many factors can influence whether a candidate wins or loses. Although the points mentioned above are brief, they can significantly impact the outcome. Factors related to growth, prosperity, self-defense, and a high GDP, among others, are also crucial, even if they aren't discussed here.

Chapter 40

Government Expenditure on National/Public Properties

Government Spending on Public Assets and Its Quality

We often notice that the money allocated for public projects doesn't always go into creating high-quality assets. Instead, due to secret agreements among leaders, officials, and vendors, some of the budgeted money ends up in their pockets. Consequently, the construction or creation of public assets, such as roads and buildings, is compromised in terms of quality. This means that these assets need more maintenance and have a shorter lifespan. Eventually, they require reconstruction, leading to a waste of the country's money.

Moreover, the deterioration of these assets happens quickly, causing them to lose their attractiveness to visitors, tourists, and the public.

Ensuring that government expenditures on public assets are used efficiently and transparently is crucial for the development and progress of a nation. When public funds are misappropriated or misused, it not only leads to financial losses but also hinders the nation's growth.

To address this issue and build a stronger nation, there needs to be increased transparency in government spending, strict enforcement of anti-corruption measures, and accountability for those who engage in corrupt practices. Additionally, investing in the training and education of officials and contractors involved in public projects can help ensure that public funds are used effectively and that the quality of public assets is maintained over time.

SUMMARY

Ultimately, a nation's prosperity and development depend on how well its resources are managed and utilized for the benefit of its citizens. Responsible and transparent government spending is a crucial element in achieving these goals.

Chapter 41

Safeguard National Properties

Preserving National Assets

Proper maintenance of national assets built with public funds can help save future expenses. Typically, the government invests in buildings or beautifies areas to benefit society or enhance national appeal. However, over time, these assets can deteriorate if they are not properly maintained. Sometimes, those responsible for upkeep only perform superficial actions to fulfill their duties.

As a result, the funds used to create these assets, sourced from the government's limited resources, end up wasted if the public does not benefit from them. In my opinion, if these properties are not adequately maintained by the responsible authorities, there is no justification for allocating additional funds for them in the government budget.

To clarify this point, I found a report in the Hindi newspaper *Punjab Kesari* (Ludhiana Edition) dated February 23, 2021, Column 5. The report discussed a musical fountain built by the government at a cost of 5 crores over 5 years. According to the report, the fountain is now worth less than 1,000 rupees if sold for scrap.

Preserving and maintaining national assets is not

just about saving money but also about ensuring that the investments made by the government benefit the public in the long run. Neglecting these assets not only leads to financial losses but also deprives the community of valuable resources. To build a stronger nation, it's essential for responsible authorities to prioritize the maintenance of national assets, implement proper management practices, and allocate necessary funds for their upkeep. Moreover, fostering a sense of ownership and responsibility among citizens toward these assets can go a long way in ensuring their preservation and continued utility.

'कंपनी बाग में एक करोड़ रुपए से लगा म्यूजिकल फाउंटेन अब कबाड़ में एक हजार का भी नहीं बिकेगा'

अकाली-भाजपा ने 5 साल पहले 5 करोड़ खर्च कर कंपनी बाग को बनाया था सुंदर

जालंधर, 22 फरवरी (खुराना): हर शहरी की इच्छा होती है कि उसका शहर सुंदर बने और साफ-सुथरा हो परंतु सरकारों के उदासीन रवैये से आम शहरियों की यह इच्छा पूरी नहीं हो पाती। जालंधर की ही बात करें तो कभी यह शहर पंजाब का सबसे सुंदर शहर माना जाता था परंतु आज यह शहर अपना सौंदर्य खो चुका है। शहर के बीचों-बीच स्थित कंपनी बाग जिसे नेहरू गार्डन भी कहा जाता है एक ऐसा ऐतिहासिक महत्व वाला स्थान है जहां अंग्रेजों के राज में जलसे इत्यादि हुआ करते थे। कई साल तक कंपनी बाग एक सैरगाह के रूप में विकसित रहा जहां अंदरूनी शहर के हजारों लोग हर रोज खुली हवा लेने के लिए आते थे।

पंजाब में 10 साल काबिज रही अकाली-भाजपा सरकार ने भी कंपनी बाग के सौंदर्यीकरण पर 5 करोड़ रुपए खर्चे और 21 जून 2015 को तत्कालीन लोकल बॉडीज मंत्री अनिल जोशी ने नए स्वरूप वाला कंपनी बाग जालंधर निवासियों को समर्पित किया था। तब कंपनी बाग में एक करोड़ रुपए का म्यूजिकल फाउंटेन भी लगाया गया था जिससे उठती रंग-बिरंगी तरंगें देखने और मधुर संगीत लहरियों को एन्जॉय करने शहर निवासी उमड़ पड़ते थे।

करीब एक साल तक इस म्यूजिकल फाउंटेन ने अपनी सेवाएं दीं परंतु बाद में यह खराब होता गया। आज 5 साल बाद हालत यह है कि एक करोड़ रुपए का यह म्यूजिकल फाउंटेन यदि कबाड़ में बेचने जाएं तो इसका जंग लगा लोहा 1000 रुपए का भी नहीं बिकेगा। आज कंपनी बाग में म्यूजिकल फाउंटेन के नाम पर सिर्फ कुछ पाइपें, एक छोटा-सा तालाब जिसमें कीचड़ और गंदगी भरी है, रह गया है। कभी लोगों को सुकून देने वाला यह म्यूजिकल फाउंटेन आज कांग्रेस सरकार की अनदेखी के कारण कंपनी बाग पर एक धब्बा सिद्ध हो रहा है।

स्मार्ट सिटी के तहत विकसित किए जा रहे पार्कों का भी न हो यह हाल

अकाली-भाजपा द्वारा 5 करोड़ रुपए से सुधारे गए कंपनी बाग को कांग्रेस सरकार ने 3-4 साल में ही लगभग नष्ट कर दिया है। अब कांग्रेस सरकार द्वारा स्मार्ट सिटी मिशन से करोड़ों रुपए खर्च करके कई पार्कों का सुधार किया जा रहा है पर लोगों को चिंता है कि कहीं आने वाले समय में इन पार्कों पर खर्च किए गए करोड़ों रुपए भी व्यर्थ न जाएं। अगर कांग्रेस इन पार्कों को न संभाल सकी तो उनका हाल भी कंपनी बाग जैसा ही होगा, इसलिए शहरियों की मांग है कि पार्कों इत्यादि में सिर्फ हरियाली की जाए और फाउंटेन इत्यादि पर पैसे न खर्च किए जाएं क्योंकि ये सरकारों से नहीं संभाले जाते।

SUMMARY

By taking proactive measures to care for and preserve national properties, a country can both save resources and enhance the quality of life for its citizens, contributing to its overall development and prosperity.

Chapter 42

Invest in Government Properties Only When Needed

I've noticed a concerning trend where roads that were not in terrible condition are being torn down and completely rebuilt, even though they could have been used for a few more years. People believe these roads could have served the public for a bit longer. In such cases, it would be wiser to perform repair work, such as patching and filling holes, which would be less costly. The saved money could then be used to develop other areas that need attention.

Supporting this idea, I read in the Hindi newspaper Ludhiana Kesari on May 20, 2022, that the Municipal Commissioner emphasized the importance of spending public funds only when necessary and in the best interest of the community. She introduced guidelines to ensure that unnecessary or unplanned work isn't undertaken without good reason. To make this a rule, she asked for photographs of the area or road where development is requested, along with a certificate from the SE (Superintending Engineer) explaining why the work is needed. This way, the whole team would be responsible for their actions when using public funds.

She also mentioned the importance of keeping a history of these roads, documenting when the work was done and the expected lifespan of the improvements, when the tender was issued or the work order was given to a contractor. Even obtaining the consent of a Municipal Councilor or Local MLA is recommended before undertaking unnecessary work, especially when funds are limited. It has been observed in numerous cases that development work is being carried out on roads, steps, flyovers, bridges, railings, plantations, and lights that were functioning satisfactorily before being renovated, while other essential amenities in the surrounding areas are being neglected.

We've often observed that while one road is meticulously maintained—with regular patchwork—the adjacent street or area is in poor condition. Additionally, roads that are already in good shape and free of defects are sometimes rebuilt before their useful life has ended. If Special Investigation Cells were to look into these practices, they might uncover various malpractices and potentially implicate individuals of high standing under statutory laws.

In some cases, multiple applications are submitted by a group of people from the same business concern but representing themselves under different names or firms to secure government contracts. This practice, known as pooling, should be discouraged to ensure fairness and provide everyone with an equal opportunity to obtain work contracts without the interference of multiple applications from the same entity.

Chapter 43

Ensuring High-Quality Infrastructure

The quality of infrastructure is incredibly important and should never be overlooked. Various steps can be taken to ensure this, but we must acknowledge that corruption among government officials is a real concern. Often, vendors compromise on the quality of infrastructure projects with the consent of those in charge. Without going into too much detail, as we are all aware, I'd like to suggest the use of bank guarantees for every contract where quality is a concern. Requiring a bank guarantee for each contract would make those involved seriously consider the quality of their work, as the guarantee could be forfeited if the quality isn't up to par. However, after a minimum guaranteed period, these guarantees could be returned or released.

Another effective measure is to monitor how government work is distributed among vendors. Instead of consistently awarding contracts to just a few vendors, it's important to distribute work more evenly among all available vendors. When a select few consistently receive contracts, it raises questions about why they are chosen over others. This should be investigated thoroughly, except in cases where those chosen few genuinely have superior capabilities. Otherwise, the repeated selection of the same vendors may be due to corrupt practices aimed at securing frequent work for them.

Ensuring the quality of infrastructure is crucial for the development and prosperity of a nation. Poor-quality infrastructure can lead to safety issues, increased maintenance costs, and a negative impact on the quality of life for citizens.

SUMMARY

To build a stronger nation, it's essential to have robust mechanisms in place to prevent corruption and promote transparency in the allocation of government contracts. Bank guarantees can serve as a powerful tool to hold contractors accountable for delivering high-quality work. Additionally, regularly evaluating the distribution of government contracts among vendors can help prevent favoritism and promote fair competition, ultimately resulting in better infrastructure for the country.

Chapter 44

Coordination Among Departments Responsible for Creating and Maintaining National Properties

Let me explain this with an example. Imagine a road is built by one government department, like the local authority. After a short while, another department, like the electricity or telephone department, decides they need to dig up that same road to lay wires underground. This can seem like a waste of time and resources, especially if the road was recently built, maybe just 6 or 12 months ago.

In a recent case in Punjab, a cabinet minister realized that a pipeline route, meant for carrying treated wastewater to a specific location, was planned to pass through a well-constructed road used for transportation. On the other side of the river, there was a road that wasn't properly built yet, with no proper materials like metal or concrete. The Minister was wise enough to stop the digging of the good road.

This kind of coordination issue can be quite common when different departments are working on projects without considering the work done by others. Coordination among various government departments responsible for infrastructure and property creation is essential to avoid unnecessary costs, delays, and disruptions. Departments must communicate and plan together to optimize the use of resources and avoid redundant work.

Efficient coordination ensures that taxpayers' money is used wisely, projects are completed faster, and public resources are not wasted on redoing work that could have been avoided with proper planning. It contributes to the overall development and prosperity of a nation by promoting efficient use of resources and avoiding unnecessary disruptions to public services.

SUMMARY

Building a stronger nation requires effective coordination and collaboration among government departments, promoting transparency and efficiency in public projects.

(Source: *Ludhiana Kesari* - Hindi News Paper, *April 2, 2021, Column 3*)

Chapter 45

Save Interest on International Loans

International loans can be valuable sources of funding for a nation's development projects and infrastructure. However, the interest payments on these loans can become a significant burden on a country's finances if not managed carefully. To build a stronger nation, it's essential to explore strategies to save on interest payments for international loans.

The first effort towards this achievement is to negotiate skillfully while securing a loan with lower interest rates, longer repayment periods, and flexible terms. This can result in substantial savings over the life of the loan. Further, relying on a single source for international loans can limit negotiation power. Diversifying sources and seeking loans from multiple institutions or countries can lead to more competitive terms.

Early Repayment: When a nation's financial situation improves, consider early repayment of loans, especially those with high interest rates. This can reduce the overall interest paid over the life of the loan.

Utilize Grants and Aid: Seek grants and aid packages that do not require repayment. While these may not replace loans entirely, they can reduce the need for borrowing, ultimately lowering interest costs.

Optimum use of such international loans for projects

that stimulate economic growth can generate additional revenue, making it easier to service the debt and cover interest payments. Ensure accountability in managing international loans to prevent misuse of funds at any level.

Refinancing: Monitor the financial markets for opportunities to refinance existing loans at more favorable terms when interest rates are low.

Nations that maintain strong creditworthiness can negotiate better terms for loans. This can be achieved through responsible fiscal management, reducing debt levels, and improving the overall economic environment.

One more thing that should be taken care of is monitoring exchange rates both at the time of availing such a loan as well as at the time when this loan is being repaid. An intelligent hedging strategy can mitigate the impact of currency fluctuations on interest payments.

SUMMARY

Saving on interest payments for international loans is an essential aspect of building a financially stable and prosperous nation. By employing strategic financial management, negotiating favorable terms, and diversifying funding sources, countries can minimize the financial burden of debt servicing. These savings can then be redirected toward critical development projects, ultimately contributing to the nation's growth and well-being.

Chapter 46

Reduce Administrative Government Expenditure

Smart Strategies for Reducing Government Expenditure

Efficient management of government expenditure is a crucial component in the path toward building a stronger nation. Governments worldwide face the challenge of balancing their budgets while fulfilling their obligations to citizens. In this context, reducing government expenditure is a strategic approach to ensure that resources are allocated effectively and public finances remain sustainable. A few strategies, although not exhaustive, can be understood from the following:

Prioritizing Spending: The first step in reducing government expenditure is to prioritize spending. Governments should focus on funding essential services such as healthcare, education, infrastructure, and security while trimming down on less critical areas.

Streamlining Bureaucracy: Reducing bureaucracy can significantly cut costs. This can be achieved by merging redundant government departments, reducing the number of public servants, and implementing digital solutions to streamline processes.

Efficient Procurement Practices: Governments often spend significant amounts on procurement. Implementing transparent and reasonably priced procurement practices can save money by getting the best value for taxpayer money.

Eliminating Waste and Fraud: Vigorous auditing and anti-corruption measures can help identify and eliminate wasteful spending and fraud within the government.

Public-Private Partnerships (PPPs): Participation of private sector expertise through PPPs can reduce the financial burden on the government while improving the quality, control, and efficiency of public services.

Reviewing Subsidies: Eliminating elements of fraud and middlemen, while providing benefits to various industries. Periodically reviewing and targeting these subsidies to those in genuine need can result in significant savings.

Investing in Technology: Embracing technology can lead to cost savings through automation, improved data management, and reduced paperwork.

Strategic Budgeting: Implementing performance-based budgeting can help ensure that taxpayer money is allocated to programs that deliver tangible results.

SUMMARY

Reducing government expenditure is not about cutting essential services or compromising the welfare of citizens. Instead, it's about making government operations more efficient, eliminating waste, and ensuring that taxpayer dollars are used wisely. By implementing these strategies, governments can achieve fiscal responsibility while continuing to meet the needs of their citizens, ultimately contributing to the development and prosperity of the nation.

C. Administrative/ Government Sector – Reforms

Keep the responsibilities of government staff intact even after retirement for the work they carried out during their tenure. If any lapse is found in their role, disciplinary action should be taken.

Chapter 47

Control Corruption

Intentional delays in decision-making can also be a form of corruption. When significant time passes, there is a loss of interest or urgency in the matter. Various investigations are carried out by the relevant departments to probe into cases of corruption, but these are unnecessarily delayed. These delays are often used to sideline the issue, making it less noticeable and seemingly less blameworthy for the individuals involved. In many cases, delays in work are not viewed as serious faults warranting strict penalties.

Bribery is an insect that eats away justice and government revenue.

Broadly speaking, bribery occurs for two reasons:

1. To convert wrong things into right ones.
2. To get the right things done quickly and easily within the byelaws.

I believe the first type of corruption, or bribery, should be unequivocally eliminated without hesitation. This form of corruption poses a significant threat to both society and the nation's well-being and must not be tolerated at any level, even if the wrongdoer holds a position of great influence or authority within society.

As for the second form of corruption, I consider it less detrimental, although it cannot be ignored as a social ill. This kind of corruption often takes the form of a "facilitation fee," paid to expedite tasks for our convenience. Upon closer examination, we may realize that we frequently pay extra for such conveniences and do not perceive it as a bribe. For instance, in the past, we used to handle all our tasks ourselves to fulfill our needs. However, over time, the system evolved, and we began delegating tasks to agents or other agencies. We willingly pay a premium to get a railway reservation through an agent rather than enduring long queues at the railway station, thus saving our time and energy. Similarly, for ongoing building construction, we prefer to hire watchmen, supervisors, and others rather than sacrificing our time and potential income from our jobs or businesses, which was not the case in the past. The emergence of "food courts" as an alternative to home cooking is another instance of this evolving trend.

One advantage of such "facilitation fees" is that the additional funds remain in circulation, stimulating the market and supporting various industries. Furthermore, the scale of this type of corruption is relatively modest. Nevertheless, it is possible to transform this social ill into an opportunity. How?

Those individuals seeking convenience and rapid results could officially opt for the second category within the respective department and reap the benefits. A portion of the extra fee collected would be allocated to the staff responsible for handling the transaction, while the remainder would contribute to the department's revenue. Crucially, this special work would be carried out by the department's staff during their off-hours to prevent disruptions to routine operations.

This approach allows staff to earn extra income officially by providing additional services, while everyday tasks remain unaffected.

Here are some more key strategies that can help combat corruption:

> It starts with political will and leadership, strengthening legal frameworks, ensuring that law enforcement is free from political interference, and encouraging ethical behavior in all sectors of society. All these factors would help control the wrong systems prevailing almost everywhere.

Decentralization of official powers may prove to be a milestone toward such elimination.

Transparency and accountability in the execution of any work with digitalization instead of manual work lead to the distribution of powers. Utilize technology, such as blockchain and data analytics, to increase transparency in financial transactions and procurement processes.

Implement e-governance solutions to minimize face-to-face interactions with government officials. The more public services are online, the fewer opportunities there are for corruption.

Corruption also arises when the prevailing system allows the use of inferior quality materials in government assets, excess billings of expenses, intentional delays in public works, or making unauthorized/wrong payments. In such cases within any government department, the whole team contributes to spreading bribery, ignoring the public interest.

Many times, corruption occurs due to unnecessary tendering of works while the existing system is running smoothly. Sometimes, to create the scope for such corruption, changes of the earlier vendors or agencies are carried out. The purpose remains only to generate bribes from such changes.

International cooperation can also be sought to collaborate with international organizations and other countries to combat cross-border corruption.

Shortage of Liquidity with Small Denominations

As much as possible, hindrances should be created in the circulation of bribes by keeping a liquidity crunch of currency with lower denominations in the hands of the public. If a nation succeeds in these two aspects, I am of the affirmed opinion that such a nation would be greatly relieved from this social evil. Further, if cash bribes might not be eliminated, their value should be reduced to a lower quantum. The amount of the bribe varies based on the value of the work, often favoring some individuals while disregarding others who are equally qualified for the same task.

Bribes in kind generally come with their own limitations. This involves the transfer of ownership rights for valuable assets, such as immovable property or vehicles. Such transfers must go through the relevant government department, which has specific procedures, including verifying the identity of the transferor.

From my understanding, these legal processes are less susceptible to manipulation compared to private offices, where changes can be made at any level, from the lowest to the highest. Controlling corruption in a country is a complex and challenging task that requires a multi-faceted approach involving government institutions, civil society, and the general public.

SUMMARY

It's important to note that combating corruption is an ongoing process that requires sustained efforts from all segments of society. Additionally, the specific strategies and approaches may vary from one country to another, depending on the unique challenges and circumstances each nation faces.

Chapter 48

Mitigate Opportunities for Litigations

Avoiding Disputes in Government Projects

In the Public Works Department, there's a higher chance of disputes compared to other departments, which often leads to legal issues. From my experience, I've seen many vendors or contractors file claims even after receiving full payment as per the contract. When they face delays or issues with payment, they see it as an opportunity to take the matter to the High Courts, starting legal proceedings. This can result in a significant waste of time, focus, and money for the government body involved. If the court rules against the department, it can lead to financial losses or further legal battles with appeals and writ petitions.

Another crucial point to consider when legal proceedings begin is having all the necessary records and handling the case intelligently. To prevent such legal disputes and protect the interests of the government department, it's essential to eliminate any possible opportunities for vendors or contractors to raise legal issues. This would be beneficial for the department.

Chapter 49

Maximize Output from Government Employees

Enhancing the Efficiency of Government Employees

Just as honesty is crucial for government employees, so is dedication to their duties. Punctuality is essential, and senior officers setting a good example by being on time can significantly influence this. If work consistently piles up, extending duty hours might become necessary. I believe this would not pose a problem for most departments, except those handling sensitive matters.

If necessary, work should also be done on leave days to complete pending tasks without interruptions. Sometimes, leaving work because regular hours are over can end up taking more time when resumed after a break. Often, working overtime or on weekends becomes essential, both for the public's benefit and the department's own interests.

Suggestions

Implement Time-Efficient Approaches. This can help reduce pending work in government departments.

Work output can be increased in two ways:

(a) Devoting more time to the job.
(b) Achieving higher output within a set timeframe.

The key to achieving more in less time lies in optimizing the workflow and actions involved in performing the job. **More can be found in my other book exclusively on the aspect of time management, i.e., TIME MANAGEMENT – HOW?**

Chapter 50

Government Deadlines and Compliance with Extensions

It's beneficial when the government addresses the real problems faced by the public and allows more time to comply with regulations. However, this should not be a constant practice. Occasionally, even government employees may request additional time by exaggerating minor issues, possibly due to a lack of motivation or other reasons. Those in charge should verify if these claims are valid.

If extending the deadline is still necessary, the government should announce it at an appropriate time—not too early, to avoid causing complacency, and not too late, when the work is nearly complete. Announcing it too early can waste both the public's time and the government's resources.

In simple terms, extending deadlines should be done wisely and only when really needed. This way, both the government and the public can benefit.

Chapter 51

Surprise Visits by Higher Authorities

Sometimes, important figures such as Ministers or high-ranking officials visit various locations to see things firsthand. However, if these visits are planned in advance, the purpose of the visit can be compromised. The team at the location being visited will often prepare everything meticulously to create a favorable impression.

To make these inspections more effective, they should be done without telling anyone in advance. This way, the people in charge can see the real situation without things being changed just for their visit.

In simple words, surprise visits by important people should be a surprise, so they can see things as they really are and make better decisions.

Chapter 52

Performance-Based System

Addressing Performance Issues with Employees

When some employees don't do their work properly or don't try to learn what they need for their job, there should be consequences. They could either be given a lower position or, if possible, be encouraged to consider early retirement.

Some employees hold higher-ranking jobs but can't perform their duties properly, so someone else has to do it for them. This isn't fair to the public or the department they work in, so something needs to be done about it. If there is no action, it would be unfair to the public. Sometimes, managers or other officers who aren't good at their jobs end up bothering innocent people for no good reason. So, it's important to make sure everyone is doing their job properly. This ensures benefits for both the public and the department, and it prevents innocent individuals from being unfairly treated.

Chapter 53

Streamlining Work by Eliminating Unnecessary Steps and Procedures

In this part, I want to talk about two things together. Firstly, we need to get rid of things at work that are not useful to us. And secondly, we should be willing to change how we work when needed.

Sometimes, at work, things can be so complicated that no one feels comfortable suggesting a better way. They worry that if they try something new, it might go wrong, and they'll be in trouble. This happens a lot in government offices, more than in private companies. In many government offices, people end up doing the same work twice without getting any benefit out of it. They keep doing things the old way because they're afraid that changing it might lead to problems, and they'd be blamed for it.

Just removing stuff that doesn't help isn't enough. We also need to give people liberty to try different ways to do their work if the situation calls for it. So, organizations should be ready to change their old ways when it makes sense.

SUMMARY

In short, systems are good, but we should always look for better ways to do things. Systems are made by people, and people aren't perfect, so mistakes can happen. Being flexible and open to change can help us do our work better.

Chapter 54

Review of Holidays in Government Departments

Making Government Holidays More Efficient

In addition to national festivals and important days, government employees should be granted shorter leaves, such as two or three hours, as needed, particularly on days we remember our national heroes.

We should determine the minimum days and hours government offices should work in a year, both for the national government and state governments. Once the minimum working days and common holidays are decided, states can have some flexibility to decide their own holidays. However, we should try to keep things balanced between the states and the central government to help the country run smoothly without too many disruptions.

If a new holiday is to be added, it should fit within the planned working schedule. We shouldn't compromise on this because it can cause problems for the public, government departments, and the whole country. Remember, the people who work are as crucial as the country's other resources, such as money, nature, and land.

Additionally, having fewer leave days can help to maintain

smooth work flow, and it's important for the government to ensure a balanced approach between work and holidays.

There are numerous examples of top leaders who work 14 to 16 hours a day for their nation, often celebrating festivals minimally and remaining dedicated to their duties. An appropriate example in this regard is Indian Prime Minister Shri Narendra Modi, who partially worked even on the day of his mother's sad demise. Not only this, but he also requested all the ministers, politicians, and other bureaucrats not to leave their respective work and approach him for condolence except a message. This demonstrates the spirit as well as the importance of the work and dedication towards the nation.

It was a message to the whole government machinery and others that one must remain present in his office for at least 10 to 15 days.

(Source – *Punjab Kesari*, dt. 31-12-2022 Page No. 1, Column 2 and from *Tribune*).

Bereaved Modi opens train link, chairs meet

Amit Cowper and Joydeep Thakur

letters@hindustantimes.com

"A glorious century rests at the feet of God... In Maa, I have always felt that trinity... the journey of an ascetic, the symbol of a selfless Karmayogi and a life committed to values..."

GANDHINAGAR/KOLKATA: Prime Minister Narendra Modi led the last rites of his mother Heeraben, who died early morning at the age of 99, and returned to work hours later, flagging off a key train link in West Bengal and chairing a meeting of the National Ganga Council via video conference.

Heeraben was undergoing treatment at the UN Mehta hospital in Ahmedabad and passed away at 3.30am, said a medical bulletin. She is survived by five sons and a daughter. Her last rites were performed at a crematorium in Gandhinagar around 9.30am in the presence of Modi, his brothers, and other family members.

"A glorious century rests at the feet of God... In Maa, I have always felt that trinity, which contains the journey of an ascetic, the symbol of a selfless Karmayogi and a life committed to values. When I met her on her 100th birthday, she said one thing, which is always remembered that work with intelligence, live life with purity, that is, work with intelligence and live life with purity," Modi tweeted.

Heeraben lived in Raysan village in Gandhinagar with the PM's younger brother Pankaj. On Friday morning, the Prime Minister first went to her residence in Raysan, and then carried the bier with her mortal remains to the Muktidham crematorium in Gandhinagar.

By 11.30am, Modi was back at work. Through video conference, he flagged off West Bengal's first Vande Bharat Express between Howrah and Jalpaiguri, as well as the Joka-Taratala stretch of the Kolkata Metro.

"I was supposed to be with you all today. But because of personal reasons I have not been able to come. For this, I want yours, and Bengal's forgiveness. Today is an opportunity to salute the sacred land of Bengal and the historic city of Kolkata," he said.

West Bengal chief minister Mamata Banerjee, who was at the event, condoled Heeraben's death. "Today is a sad day for you (Modi) personally and it is a great loss ... There is no substitute for mother. Your mother is our mother also," she said. "You were supposed to come to West Bengal but because of the demise of your mother you couldn't reach. But you have reached virtually. I would request to make the program cut short and take rest because you are coming after cremation," she added.

Modi invoked *Vande Mataram*, the song on which the name of the train is based on, and the birthplace of its creator, Bankim Chandra Chatterjee.

"Today's Vande Bharat train was launched from the land where Vande Mataram slogan was coined. The launch date of December 30 is significant as Netaji Subhas Chandra Bose had hoisted the tricolour in Andaman and Nicobar Islands on this day in 1943... In the 21st century, for rapid development of the country, growth and reform of railways is essential. A nationwide campaign is underway to transform rail-

continued on →19

(D) SOCIAL REFORMS

Chapter 55

Promote Internal Peace

A country that enjoys internal peace over time definitely has an edge in numerous benefits compared to other nations facing such problems. A significant part of government assets in terms of time, concentration, money, and administrative forces are lost in solving disputes among states, regions, castes, or other groups. If such disturbances occur frequently in a country, how can they spare the time to plan for growth, international reputation, or the social welfare of its citizens? Opposition to policies that lead to such protests or agitations is not discouraged, but other methods of opposition are always preferable. Round table discussions with the concerned government section, mediation through media, or within a set protocol acceptable to both parties and led by the Constitution of a country should be followed so that the rest of the country can continue their work as usual.

Avoid Inter-Citizen Disputes

Family disputes, matrimonial/relationship disputes, or other inter-citizen conflicts should be avoided to the maximum extent. This refers to both civil and criminal nature disputes. If every citizen does their best to avoid situations and still, if they happen, tries to resolve them within their close circle instead of approaching the police station or court, the whole government machinery would find time to maintain other disciplines. I have seen when mega camps to resolve such disputes are organized by the government with the help of the police and others associated with such forums, how much time, energy, absence from their other duties, financial expenses, etc., go in vain just to bring both parties to the table of compromise? From a police constable to the level of Commissioner of Police or other dignitaries, they all have to involve themselves in such cases.

SUMMARY

Internal problems can hinder a country's progress compared to those without them. When protests or demonstrations happen in a country, they can disrupt progress and lead to conflicts between the authorities and the protesters. Minimizing these situations benefits the country.

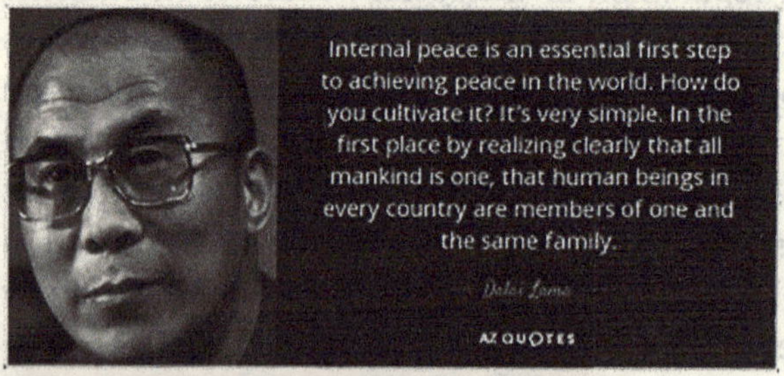

Chapter 56

Role of Public

The role of the public in building a nation is pivotal and multifaceted. The collective efforts, values, and contributions of a nation's citizens play a fundamental role in shaping its identity, progress, and development. Active participation in the democratic process through voting, voicing concerns, and engaging in public discourse is essential. Citizens have the power to elect representatives who can enact policies that align with the nation's interests. A careful understanding of the long-term vision of the selection of national representatives can determine the path of the growth of a nation. This is a crucial moment when the public is in full power and supposed to set the future for themselves, the next generation, and the selected candidates.

Similarly, the protection of the environment is crucial for the sustainability of a nation. Responsible resource management, conservation efforts, and sustainable practices are responsibilities of the public.

Respecting the rule of law and adhering to societal norms are essential for maintaining order and stability within a nation. Citizens must play their part in upholding these principles. However, if any issue arises, suggestions for improvement must be passed on to the respective departments.

Thoughts of Dignitaries

Legendary saints are not very concerned about things like industries, businesses, money, or material growth in a country. Instead, they focus on creating harmony and peace among the people. They teach their followers to be good and kind to others, and they believe this is what makes a nation great.

While they don't completely ignore the economic side of things, they believe that a nation's worth is based on the abilities of its people, their good behavior, how they treat others, and their respect for God. They aim for peace, prosperity, and equality for everyone.

These saints think that true greatness lies in the way people treat each other and their commitment to living in peace and harmony. They believe that when people are good and kind, the country automatically becomes self-reliant and prosperous.

So, for them, the key to a strong nation isn't just about money or industries, but about how people behave and treat one another.

SUMMARY

The public plays an indispensable role in nation-building by actively participating in the democratic process, fostering community cohesion, contributing to the economy, upholding ethical values, and working collectively to address societal challenges. Ultimately, the strength and vitality of a nation depend on the active engagement and responsible actions of its citizens.

Chapter 57

Combat Black Money

No nation is interested in generating black money, or unaccounted money, within its boundaries unless there are visionary benefits ahead. This money does not contribute to the national GDP. The circulation of transactions from this remains unaccounted for and is not part of the record.

The second impact of this money that affects both the public and the nation is the infrequent circulation of such wealth, which should be restricted to fewer uses. The government discourages such money as it remains idle for extended periods; neither the owner uses it nor can the government integrate it into its commonwealth

Black money provides notional benefits more than real ones. While a person might feel pleased to possess such valuable assets, the actual use of that money remains limited and ultimately unsatisfying. Many times, it has been seen that such money is expensed with less understanding than white money because there may be a hurry to invest it somewhere. White money is only invested for good reasons, while black money is generally invested in unlawful activities.

One more benefit of white money is that the owner knows the calculated figure with him, subject to the speculative items or value of immovable properties. In the case of black money, this does not happen as accurately.

One more benefit of white money is that the owner of this property knows the calculated figure with him subject to the speculative items or value of immovable properties. In the Black money case, this does not so accurately happen.

Therefore, people should avoid holding easy money or cash to the extent possible. It is preferable to keep funds in banks after paying the necessary taxes and liabilities. If you choose to hold cash, you must exercise particular care in its retention, as this is often less required in other situations. We are aware of the many disadvantages associated with keeping earnings in cash or other physical forms. While some individuals manage their funds in this way and arrange for their safety, this approach can sometimes lead to significant issues. For instance, explaining such holdings can become challenging during searches or surveys conducted by government departments. These factors vary depending on the circumstances and their impact may also be different in each situation.

Experience has shown that investments made with cash funds are often less careful compared to those made through other payment methods.

On the contrary, routing all financial transactions through banks or electronic media provides benefits that counteract the disadvantages of holding cash. Bank transactions are generally more accountable and verifiable by both government departments and private organizations. One major reason people create cash funds is to evade taxes or other government duties. In some countries, accumulating black money becomes a necessity to cover expenses like bribes or corruption, which cannot be easily addressed through official channels other than cash.. Without going further into detail, I am still of the strong opinion that black money does not benefit anyone, neither the person themselves nor their organization, and also not any country whose GDP comes only from accountable transactions from any sector.

I am aware of many cases where surveys or searches have been conducted by various central or state government departments in different organizations. Initially, these business organizations or service providers viewed tax payments as a burdensome and unwanted outgo of funds due to the outcomes of such inspections, causing concern over the tax liabilities resulting from these surveys or raids. Typically, the tax amount due includes the basic tax, plus interest and penalties on the concealed or avoided income. However, the frequency of such inspections seems to be rising, not only in India but also in other countries. Whenever a meeting is held with some business entrepreneurs, I always say, "SO FAR I HAVE NOT SEEN A PERSON IN MY LIFE WHO HAS BECOME POOR AFTER PAYING TAXES TO THE GOVT."

Further, if one is patriotic, then the payment of taxes helps the country in the creation of infrastructure and many other things for its people. Even in one's toughest financial days, a person with white income survives longer compared to those who have black money in equal amounts.

This can be further explained with another example. Suppose there are two people, let's say Person A and Person B, earning a good amount of money from the same line of business but having entirely different opinions about the payment of taxes to the government. Person A likes to pay all the taxes as per the rules and regulations of the law. On the contrary, Person B has the opinion of non-payment of taxes as it would be a total loss to him if he pays taxes. So, he always avoids paying taxes by making many manipulations in his records.

At this point, a leading news magazine has conducted a survey that is often considered representative of the industry or business organizations. This magazine is a popular choice among individuals involved in business, both directly and indirectly, as it features valuable and up-to-date information from various government and private departments, along with appealing photoshoots of models. Overall, this magazine was known for its reliable content and glamorous look for every industry, which is why it has maintained its number one position in the market for many years.

One day, this magazine initiated a survey targeting individuals of equal social status for a specific purpose. When they approached Person A, he was on a holiday tour with his beautiful wife and two lovely kids. Anyhow, they fixed the next appointment with him a day after he was to return home. After reaching home, a meeting was held where he informed the survey team about everything, they required from him. He also said that he has about 75 to 80 lakhs bank balance in the form of FDs from where he earns regular interest as a side income and he does not fear any leakage of valuable assets from his business as everything is on record. So, his staff easily handles the business in his absence. Meanwhile, the survey team could not stop themselves from narrating some content about Person B who is also doing almost the same volume of business as Person A but was not so satisfied in terms of his business as well as his personal life. Further, Person B was also having almost 20% more money than Person A as he avoids paying taxes to the government. Going further in detail, the said team found that to avoid taxes, Person B has to make a number of adjustments in his books of account every time, visit personally to collect payments from customers due to cash payments, give full-time duty at the business either himself or his wife due to unaccounted transactions in the business. Simultaneously, caring for the home where he used to keep his hard-earned money and other valuable belongings earned from the business becomes a need that can't be ignored by his family. This is the reason that he most of the time remains busy doing all the above along with some fear of being checked by any government department. For all this, he also has to incur some expenses for the manipulation of accounts, the safety of the wealth, etc. This was the story of that time of both individuals with a difference in style of living life.

After some months, the provincial government of that state announced some benefits in the form of subsidies to all business entities of their trade, subject to the submission of certain records or information as per their requirement.

As we came to know later, Person A was entitled to a good benefit in the form of a subsidy because he had everything on record, whereas Person B lost his right to avail of this benefit from the relevant scheme due to a lack of required data of the business.

Exception: The only exception to this, in my opinion, is when a country's industry exports goods to another country. In such cases, every possible demand from the importer should be accommodated in the billing. A question may arise: if the cost of production is fully accounted for, how can the sale be made at a lower value? Although this presents a challenge for the exporter and their country (e.g., China), efforts can be made to address the issue for the benefit of both parties. For example, a two-tier billing system might be implemented: one for the exporter's home country and another for the importing country, with a fixed percentage difference between the two.

Suggestions

To curb this practice, a government should allow individuals to deposit their black money into banks by paying taxes at the rate applicable to their income tax return from the previous year. However, if the deposited amount would have pushed them into a higher tax bracket in last year's return, the tax rate should be adjusted accordingly. Those who have never filed their ITR can deposit any sum by paying tax at the highest rate. In both cases, questions of WHY, WHAT, HOW, FROM WHERE should not be asked by the income tax officials. This would prove to be the best way of detecting blocked money in the economic system of the country. However, necessary conditions might be imposed, such as:

1. Minimum period of such deposit.
2. Assessees must be actual income earners.

SUMMARY

To the extent possible, black money should be avoided. Even less money that remains after the payment of respective taxes provides more materialistic benefits than those higher amounts which have been concealed from the government.

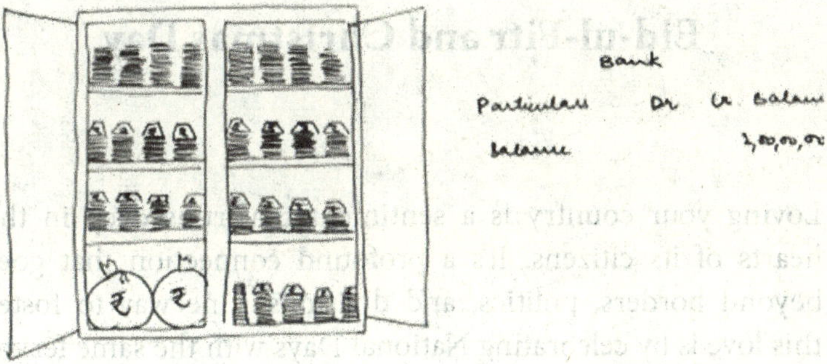

Chapter 58

Celebrate National Days like Diwali, Eid-ul-Fitr and Christmas Day

Loving your country is a sentiment that runs deep in the hearts of its citizens. It's a profound connection that goes beyond borders, politics, and divisions. One way to foster this love is by celebrating National Days with the same fervor and spirit as other major festivals like Diwali, Eid-ul-Fitr, and Christmas. This approach will not only strengthen the bond among citizens but also have a significant psychological effect on their minds, promoting unity, patriotism, and a sense of belonging.

Promoting Unity

By infusing the spirit of these festivals into National Day celebrations, we can bridge divides within our society. Festivals often emphasize the values of love, harmony, and compassion. When these values become the centerpiece of our National Day festivities, we send a powerful message that transcends political differences and unites us as one people, one nation.

Strengthening Patriotism

Celebrating National Days like Diwali, Eid-ul-Fitr, or Christmas can strengthen our sense of patriotism. Just as these festivals remind us of our cultural roots and religious beliefs, a National Day celebration that captures the essence of our country's history, struggles, and achievements can reinforce our collective identity and what we stand for as a nation. This reinforcement of national pride is essential for the development and progress of any country.

Fostering a Sense of Belonging

Festivals also create a sense of belonging. When we participate in communal activities and celebrations, we feel connected to those around us. Similarly, celebrating National Day like Diwali, Eid-ul-Fitr, or Christmas can make every citizen feel like an integral part of their country's journey. It fosters a sense of belonging and encourages people to contribute positively to their nation's growth and development.

Psychological Impact

The psychological effect of celebrating National Day in this manner is profound. It will nurture a positive mindset, as citizens will begin to associate their love for their country with the same warmth and joy they experience during festivals. It will create a collective consciousness that encourages people to act in the best interests of their nation and fellow citizens.

SUMMARY

Incorporating the spirit of Diwali, Eid-ul-Fitr, and Christmas into our National Day celebrations can work wonders in promoting love for our country. It strengthens unity, reinforces patriotism, fosters a sense of belonging, and has a positive psychological impact on our minds. Let us celebrate our National Day with the same enthusiasm and fervor as these festivals, for in doing so, we not only celebrate our nation but also the values and principles that bind us together as its proud citizens.

Chapter 59

Address Special Privileges and Their Impact (Nothing Should Be Free)

People from different backgrounds, like different religions, colors, and societies, shouldn't ask for extra advantages that only benefit a few. When a nation offers equal chances to everyone, it's important for all citizens to follow the same rules and not make things difficult by asking for extra benefits for specific groups. However, sometimes special privileges might be necessary, like in the case of natural disasters or other exceptional situations. In those cases, the government might provide financial help, social support, medical assistance, education, or other basic needs to help those affected get back on their feet. But these special privileges should only be temporary and not last too long. If they do, people might stop trying to be self-reliant and rely too much on the government.

To put it differently, it is my belief that retirees who receive pensions should be given certain tasks, such as desk work or supervisory roles, for a few hours each day as part of their pension arrangement. However, I support the idea of providing a pension to the surviving spouse of a deceased employee. It would be beneficial to establish some guidelines for this practice. Involvement in light work during the pension period can have a positive impact on the retired employees' morale, self-confidence, and self-sufficiency. Simultaneously, it can contribute to their overall well-being and mental acuity. This approach could also foster social reforms by redirecting attention from idle conversations at home or on street corners to productive official work. If it's not deemed suitable for an entire retirement, at the very least, this practice should continue for the first ten years. Comparatively, in the private sector, entrepreneurs often work well into their 80s and even 90s. Therefore, there is no reason why the government sector shouldn't consider a similar approach.

Many wise and experienced individuals have also advised against such benefits. They've talked about how these policies can harm the people who receive them in the long run. Plus, no nation can afford to provide special privileges forever, especially when many different communities are asking for help, and resources are limited. A few articles published in the newspapers are also attached hereunder.

In general, I don't oppose a government's charitable efforts to uplift disadvantaged segments of society. However, providing assistance should be a reciprocal process, encouraging individuals to contribute in return. This not only stimulates the pursuit of additional avenues for income but also ensures the judicious use of limited resources in areas that might not be of utmost importance. Nevertheless, the notion of unconditionally receiving without any corresponding effort may not serve the long-term interests of the deserving beneficiaries. Hence, if something is provided without any cost, there should be an accompanying expectation of engagement in productive activities. This approach helps prevent the development of a habit of non-productivity and encourages a sense of responsibility and contribution to the nation.

आरक्षण बन गया अफीम की गोली

भारत में जातीय आरक्षण अफीम की गोली बन चुका है। हर राजनीतिक दल चाहता है कि वह जातीय आधार पर थोक वोट सेंत-मेत में कबाड़ ले। इस समय दो प्रदेशों में जातीय आरक्षण को लेकर काफी दंगल मचा हुआ है। एक है, छत्तीसगढ़ और दूसरा है-उत्तरप्रदेश! पहले में कांग्रेस की सरकार है और दूसरे में भाजपा की सरकार। लेकिन दोनों तुली हुई हैं कि 50 प्रतिशत की संवैधानिक सीमा को तोड़कर आरक्षण को 76 प्रतिशत और अन्य पिछड़ा वर्ग तक बढ़ा दिया जाए। बिहार तथा कुछ अन्य प्रांतों में भी इस तरह के विवादों ने तूल पकड़ लिया है।

डा. वेदप्रताप वैदिक

जहां तक छत्तीसगढ़ का सवाल है, उसकी सरकार ने विधानसभा में ऐसे विधेयक को पारित कर दिया है, जो 58 प्रतिशत आरक्षण को बढ़ाकर 76 प्रतिशत कर देता है। आर्थिक दृष्टि से पिछड़ों के लिए सिर्फ 4 प्रतिशत आरक्षण रखा गया है। इस नई प्रस्तावित आरक्षण-व्यवस्था के पीछे न तो कोई ठोस आंकड़े हैं और न ही तर्क हैं। सितंबर 2022 में प्रदेश के उच्च न्यायालय ने एक फैसले में साफ-साफ कहा था कि 50 प्रतिशत से अधिक आरक्षण देना असंवैधानिक है।

सर्वोच्च न्यायालय ने भी अपने एक फैसले में कहा था कि सीमा से अधिक आरक्षण देना हो तो उसके लिए उसे तीन पैमानों पर पहले नापा जाना चाहिए। यानी उनकी आर्थिक-शैक्षणिक स्थिति, उन्हें आरक्षण की जरूरत है या नहीं और वह उन्हें दिया जा सकता है या नहीं? यह जांचने के लिए बाकायदा एक सर्वेक्षण आयोग बनाया जाना चाहिए। इन सब शर्तों को दर-किनार करके सभी राज्य आरक्षण की आनन-फानन बढ़ा रहे हैं। छत्तीसगढ़ में तो राज्यपाल अनसूइया उइके पर राजनीतिक प्रहार किए जा रहे हैं कि वे भाजपा के इशारे पर इस विधेयक पर दस्तखत नहीं कर रही हैं।

यदि यह सही होता तो उ.प्र. के मुख्यमंत्री स्थानीय चुनावों में अन्य पिछड़ा वर्ग को आरक्षण देने पर क्यों अड़े हुए हैं? योगी के इस फैसले का विरोध अखिलेश और मायावती भी कर रहे हैं, क्योंकि उनके वोट बैंक में इस फैसले से सेंध लग सकती है। योगी ने अपने उच्च न्यायालय के आरक्षण-विरोधी फैसले से असहमति व्यक्त की है और कहा है कि जब तक इस आरक्षण का प्रावधान नहीं होगा, उ.प्र. में स्थानीय चुनाव नहीं होंगे। उ.प्र. सरकार ने न्यायालय की अपेक्षा को पूरा करने के लिए एक जातीय सर्वेक्षण आयोग का प्रावधान भी कर दिया है।

अर्थात सरकारें कांग्रेस की हों, भाजपा की हों, जदयू की हों या कम्युनिस्टों की हों, किसी की हिम्मत नहीं है कि वह जातीय आरक्षण का विरोध करे यानी वे डा. आंबेडकर की इच्छा को पूरी करते अर्थात जात-आधारित आरक्षण को 10 साल से ज्यादा चलने न देते।

छत्तीसगढ़ की राज्यपाल तो स्वयं आदिवासी महिला हैं। वे आदिवासियों के हितार्थ बहुत कुछ पहल कर रही हैं। वे यदि इस अंधाधुंध जातीय आरक्षण पर शांति से विचार करने के लिए कह रही हैं तो उसमें गलत क्या है? हमारी अदालतें भी आरक्षण के विरुद्ध नहीं हैं लेकिन वे अंधाधुंध रेवड़ियां बांटने का विरोध कर रही हैं तो नेताओं को जरा अपने थोक वोटों के लालच पर कुछ लगाम लगानी चाहिए या नहीं?

dr.vaidik@gmail.com

आरक्षण का आधार सिर्फ गरीबी हो

भोपाल में कर्णी सेना ने एक अपूर्व प्रदर्शन आयोजित किया और मांग की कि सरकारी नौकरियों, चुनावों और शिक्षण संस्थाओं में, जहां भी आरक्षण की व्यवस्था है, वहां सिर्फ गरीबी के आधार पर आरक्षण दिया जाए। यह कर्णी सेना राजपूतों का संगठन है।

इसने जातीय आरक्षण के विरुद्ध सीधी आवाज नहीं उठाई है क्योंकि यह खुद ही जातीय संगठन है, लेकिन इस समय देश में जहां भी आरक्षण दिया जा रहा है, वह प्रायः जातीय आधार पर ही दिया जा रहा है। यदि सिर्फ गरीबी के आधार पर आरक्षण की व्यवस्था बन जाए तो जाति भेदभाव के बिना भी देश के सभी कमजोर लोगों को आरक्षण मिल सकता है।

डा. वेदप्रताप वैदिक

यह मांग तो भारत के कम्युनिस्टों को सबसे ज्यादा करनी चाहिए, क्योंकि कार्ल मार्क्स ने 'कम्युनिस्ट मैनिफैस्टो' में सबसे ज्यादा हिमायत इसी गरीब वर्ग की है। उन्होंने इसे सर्वहारा (प्रोलेटेरिएट) कहा है। कम्युनिस्टों की क्या कहें, देश की सभी पार्टियां थोक वोटों की गुलाम हैं। थोक वोटों का सबसे बड़ा स्रोत जातियां ही हैं।

इसीलिए देश के किसी नेता या पार्टी में इतना दम नहीं है कि वह जातीय आरक्षण का विरोध करे। बल्कि कई अन्य जातियों के नेता आजकल अपने लिए आरक्षण के आंदोलन चला रहे हैं। यदि कर्णी सेना के राजपूत लोग अपने आंदोलन में सभी जातियों को जोड़ लें (अनुसूचित जातियों को भी) तो वह सचमुच महान राष्ट्रीय आंदोलन बन सकता है। अनेक अनुसूचित लोग, जो स्वाभिमानी हैं और दूसरों की दया पर निर्भर रहना गलत मानते हैं, वे भी कर्णी सेना के साथ आ जाएंगे।

कर्णी सेना की यह मांग भी सही है कि किसी भी परिवार की सिर्फ एक पीढ़ी को आरक्षण दिया जाए ताकि अगली पीढ़ियां आत्म-निर्भर हो जाएं। कर्णी सेना की यह मांग भी उचित प्रतीत होती है कि उस कानून को वापस लिया जाए, जिसके मुताबिक किसी भी अनुसूचित व्यक्ति की शिकायत के आधार पर किसी को भी जांच किए बिना ही गिरफ्तार कर लिया जाता है।

इसमें शक नहीं है कि देश के अनुसूचितों ने सदियों से बहुत जुल्म सहे हैं और उनके प्रति न्याय होना बेहद जरूरी है लेकिन हम भारत में ऐसा समाज बनाने की भूल न करें, जो जातीय आधार पर हजारों टुकड़ों में बंटता चला जाए।

भारत और पड़ोसी देशों के तथाकथित अनुसूचित और पिछड़े लोगों को आगे बढ़ाने का उपाय जातीय आरक्षण नहीं है। उन्हें और तथाकथित ऊंची जातियों के लोगों को भी जन्म के आधार पर नहीं, जरूरत के आधार पर आरक्षण दिया जाए। यदि हम आरक्षण का आधार ठीक कर लें तो देश में समता और सम्पन्नता का भवन तो अपने आप ही खड़ा हो जाएगा।

dr.vaidik@gmail.com

SUMMARY

If the benefits provided by the government start becoming a regular part of the lives of those who receive them, it's essential for the government to rethink these privileges. A universal perception of free amenities leads to wrong habits in society. In my opinion, needs become the mother of hard work, intelligence, motivation, and success. Now, if needs are being fulfilled by default,I don't believe that people will exhibit the same spirit of work, education, or self-improvement compared to when they were meeting their needs through their own efforts. Unemployment habits may begin to develop, which is detrimental to a nation. particularly in the current scenario when all other countries are aggressively striving to reach new heights in various spheres of life.

Ultimately, if circumstances necessitate waiving certain benefits in the public interest, my suggestion is to provide those benefits but take some form of compensation in return—not by way of the price of those benefits but in the form of services of those people. This labor would contribute to the creation of national assets, rather than increasing the cost of the benefits themselves. Such a practice would not allow them to develop the habit of not struggling for their own needs and becoming entirely dependent on the nation. Even in this philosophy, particularly in a democratic country, the electoral process would not be significantly impacted in favor of a particular contesting party.

Chapter 60

Reform the Reservation System

Reducing Special Privileges and Encouraging Business Opportunities

We should limit the special privileges given to some people in jobs and education. When certain groups receive these privileges, it can make others feel like they don't have a fair chance. In some cases, this can lower the quality of services provided by government departments.

Instead of relaxing entrance requirements, we can offer other benefits. For example, we could allow these groups to have a higher age limit when applying for jobs. They could also receive extra perks or be allowed to retire later, as long as they're physically and mentally fit. These changes can help them without **compromising the quality of services.**

When it comes to education, it's okay to provide extra help up to a basic level. After that, everyone should have an equal chance. At this point, individual interests and passions matter, and everyone should be treated fairly.

We can also support these groups in different ways. We can help them start businesses, allocate shops for them, or provide financial aid for manual or semi-skilled work. These benefits might not show immediate results but can be helpful in the long run, both for them and the nation's economy. With the growth of their businesses, various kinds of jobs will naturally be created by default, and the purpose of increasing the income of the weaker section of society would be fulfilled in two ways: first, by enabling them to do business, and second, by employing others in their businesses who need these opportunities.

In the end, if special privileges are still needed, we can give people the choice between job benefits or business opportunities with government support.

SUMMARY

Providing free amenities is a good thing, especially when it benefits the entire nation rather than a select few.

Chapter 61

Build a Drugs-Free Society for a Strong Nation

The scourge of drug addiction is a pervasive problem that affects individuals, families, and communities, ultimately posing a significant threat to the overall well-being and development of a nation. Building a drug-free society is not just a moral imperative but a crucial element in nation-building. This essay explores the multifaceted role of drug addiction in the nation-building process, shedding light on its implications for public health, social cohesion, economic productivity, and overall national progress.

Public Health and Well-being

At the heart of any thriving nation is the health and well-being of its citizens. Substance abuse and addiction take a severe toll on the physical and mental health of individuals. By prioritizing drug addiction, a nation invests in the rehabilitation and recovery of its citizens, allowing them to lead healthier, more productive lives.

De-addiction programs provide individuals with the necessary support, counseling, and medical assistance to break free from the cycle of addiction. This not only improves the quality of life for those directly affected but also reduces the burden on healthcare systems, allowing resources to be allocated more efficiently.

Social Cohesion and Family Stability

Drug addiction often tears at the social fabric of communities and families. It leads to fractured relationships, child neglect, and criminal activity. By addressing drug addiction, a nation can strengthen family bonds, promote social cohesion, and reduce the strain on law enforcement and social services.

Recovery and rehabilitation programs also help individuals reintegrate into society as responsible, productive citizens, reducing recidivism and the perpetuation of a cycle of addiction.

Economic Productivity and Human Capital

A drug-free society contributes to economic productivity by ensuring that a nation's workforce is healthy and capable. Substance abuse not only impairs an individual's ability to work but also leads to absenteeism, reduced productivity, and increased workplace accidents.

National Security and Crime Reduction

A drug-free society enhances national security by reducing the demand for illegal drugs, weakening criminal networks, and decreasing the involvement of individuals in drug-related crimes. It frees up law enforcement resources to focus on more pressing issues and fosters a safer environment for all citizens.

SUMMARY

The role of drug addiction in nation-building is undeniable. It is not just a matter of curbing a social ill but a fundamental step toward fostering a healthier, more stable, and prosperous society. Nations that prioritize addressing drug addiction invest in their human capital, strengthen social bonds, and reduce the burden on healthcare and law enforcement systems.

To build a nation that stands strong and resilient, it is imperative to address drug addiction comprehensively, combining prevention, treatment, and rehabilitation efforts. A drug-free society not only benefits individuals and families but also contributes to the collective well-being, progress, and prosperity of the nation as a whole.

Chapter 62

One Nation – One Language: For Both National & International Use

Why are we spending so much time on the issue of different languages, their priorities, controversies, and making some people happy while others are unhappy? Let's put an end to these debates and accept what has been decided in our country's Parliament.

To keep our nation united, peaceful, and morally enthusiastic, we need to consider the following ideas. Many wise and learned people have emphasized the importance of having one language, specifically Hindi, spoken throughout our entire country. These individuals include Maharishi Dayanand Saraswati, Mahatma Gandhi, Ram Manohar Lohia, Sant Vinoba Bhave, Gunnar Myrdal from Sweden, Rabindranath Tagore, Alfons Vatvel from Holland, and others. This book is not just for Indian nationalists, so I believe that using only one national language in all parts of the country is a good idea. I understand that there may be opposition from people in different regions who are used to speaking their regional languages extensively. Opposition parties may also try to use this as a political opportunity against the ruling party.

Having one national language can promote unity and

understanding among citizens. It can simplify communication, reduce language barriers, and foster a sense of belonging to a single nation. However, it's essential to strike a balance between preserving regional cultures and promoting a common language for the greater good of the nation. Inclusivity and sensitivity to linguistic diversity should be considered while implementing such policies.

हिंदी कैसे बने विश्वभाषा

डा. वेदप्रताप वैदिक

हर वर्ष 10 जनवरी को विश्व हिंदी दिवस के रूप में मनाया जाता है। इस दिन के बारे में मेरे विचारों से बेहतर यह होगा कि हमारे भारतीय और विदेशी महापुरुषों और विद्वानों द्वारा हिंदी के बारे में जो कुछ कहा गया है, उसे संक्षेप में आपके लिए प्रस्तुत कर दूं।

हिन्दी द्वारा सारे भारत को एक सूत्र में पिरोया जा सकता है। मेरी आंखें वह दिन देखने के लि[illegible]स रही हैं, जब कश्मीर से कन्याकुमारी तक सब भारतीय एक ही भाषा को समझने और बोलने लगेंगे।

—महर्षि दयानन्द सरस्वती

यदि मैं तानाशाह होता तो आज ही विदेशी भाषा में शिक्षा दिया जाना बंद कर देता। सारे अध्यापकों को स्वदेशी भाषाएं अपनाने को मजबूर कर देता। जो आनाकानी करते, उन्हें बर्खास्त कर देता। मैं, पाठ्य पुस्तकों के तैयार किए जाने का इन्तजार न करता। अंग्रेजों को हम गालियां देते हैं कि उन्होंने हिन्दुस्तान को गुलाम बनाया, लेकिन उनकी अंग्रेजी भाषा के तो हम अभी तक गुलाम बने बैठे हैं।

—महात्मा गांधी

हिन्दी में मैं इसलिए लिखता और प्रवचन देता हूं क्योंकि इस भाषा में विचारों को स्पष्टता से सामने लाने की अद्भुत क्षमता है। मैं तो चाहता हूं कि देवनागरी लिपि में ही देश की सब भाषाएं लिखी जाएं। इससे दूसरी भाषाएं सीखना आसान हो जाएगा। ...केवल अंग्रेजी सीखने में जितना श्रम करना पड़ता है, उतने श्रम में हिन्दुस्तान की सभी भाषाएं सीखी जा सकती हैं। ...मैं दुनिया की सब भाषाओं की इज्जत करता हूं, परंतु मेरे देश में हिन्दी की इज्जत न हो, यह मैं नहीं सह सकता। —संत विनोबा भावे

जब एक बार शराब पीने की आदत पड़ जाती है तो किसी न किसी रूप में कानून का सहारा लेना पड़ता है। आज अंग्रेजी शराब से भी ज्यादा नुक्सान कर रही है और अंग्रेजीबन्दी शराबबन्दी से भी ज्यादा जरूरी है।

— राममनोहर लोहिया

जब तक भारतीय संसद के वाद-विवाद अंग्रेजी में चलते रहेंगे, देश की राजनीति का जनता से कोई सरोकार नहीं होगा और वह एक छोटे से वर्ग की बपौती बनकर रह जाएगी।

—गुन्नार मिर्डल (स्वीडन के प्रसिद्ध समाजशास्त्री)

विदेशी भाषा के माध्यम से शिक्षा किसी सभ्य देश में प्रदान नहीं की जाती। विदेशी भाषा के माध्यम से शिक्षा देने से छात्रों का मन विकारग्रस्त हो जाता है और वे अपने ही देश में परदेशी के समान मालूम पड़ते हैं।

—रबीन्द्रनाथ टैगोर

भारत में अनेक भाषाएं बोली जाती हैं। उन भाषाओं के बीच में अंग्रेजी कैसे सम्पर्क भाषा बन सकती है, क्या दिल्ली का रास्ता लंदन से होकर गुजरता है? अंग्रेजी अलगाव पैदा करती है, जनता और नेता के बीच, राजा और प्रजा के बीच। अंग्रेजी हटेगी तो उत्तर भारत के लोग भी दक्षिण की भाषा सीखेंगे। —आलफंस वातवेल, हालैंड

dr.vaidik@gmail.com

(Source: *Punjab Kesari*, Page 4, Column 1 & 2)

Chapter 63

Regulate Prices of Essential Goods

The Importance of Regulating Prices of Essential Goods for Nation-Building

In the journey of nation-building, there are few aspects as crucial as ensuring the well-being of its citizens. Access to essential goods and services is fundamental to the prosperity and stability of any nation. One critical component of this equation is the regulation of prices for necessary goods. Here, we explore why regulating the prices of essential items is not just a policy choice but an imperative for building a strong and resilient nation.

Economic Stability: Price stability is the cornerstone of a thriving economy. When the prices of essential goods are allowed to skyrocket unchecked, inflation can spiral out of control, eroding the purchasing power of ordinary citizens. This instability can hinder economic growth, discourage investment, and lead to financial hardship for many. Regulating prices helps maintain economic stability by keeping inflation in check.

Social Equity: A nation's strength lies in the well-being of its people. When essential goods like food, medicine, and housing become unaffordable, it widens the gap between the rich and the poor. Price regulation ensures that these necessities remain within reach for all citizens, regardless of their income level. This fosters social equity and prevents the marginalization of vulnerable populations.

Food Security: Food is not just a commodity; it is a basic human need. Ensuring a stable and affordable food supply is essential for food security, a cornerstone of national security. Price regulation in the agriculture sector helps protect farmers from exploitation while ensuring a consistent food supply for the entire nation.

Political Stability: Unchecked price increases can lead to public unrest and social discontent. History has shown that economic hardships resulting from rising prices can be a catalyst for political instability and even revolutions. Price regulation can help prevent such crises and maintain political stability.

Investor Confidence: A nation with a well-regulated market that protects consumers and ensures fair pricing is more likely to attract foreign investment. When investors see that a country values economic stability and social equity, they are more inclined to contribute to its development, creating a positive cycle of growth.

SUMMARY

In conclusion, the regulation of prices for essential goods is not merely a matter of economic policy; it is a moral and strategic imperative for nation-building. It safeguards the well-being of citizens, promotes economic stability, and contributes to social equity. To build a strong and prosperous nation, it is essential that we prioritize the regulation of prices for necessary goods as a fundamental aspect of our national strategy.

Chapter 64

Promote Affordable or Generic Medicines

If the nation is poor or developing, then traditional and cheap medical treatment should also be simultaneously promoted along with modern therapy. This would help those people who are hand-to-mouth and are not in a position to afford costly medical treatments.

If they spend their whole income on this, they would not be in a position to come forward and invest in economic development, both for themselves and for the nation.

Some might argue that if the poor man spends money on his treatment, it will still remain in public funds with the respective hospitals and others. However, I discourage this concept for two reasons. First, very few people would have the courage to take the initiative of getting such treatment. Second, if they spend a hefty amount on medicines from limited funds, they will have to rely on borrowing or other unsocial factors for other expenses, which are not good for various social reasons.

Access to affordable healthcare and medicines is vital for public health. When the prices of essential medicines or medical services soar, it can lead to dire consequences. Price regulation in the healthcare sector ensures that necessary treatments and medications remain accessible to all, ultimately contributing to better public health outcomes.

Chapter 65

Long-Term Visionary Approach – Not Penny Wise, Pound Foolish

In the concept of nation-building, a "Penny Wise, Pound Foolish" approach refers to having long visionary thinking towards one's lifestyle, humanity, maintaining cordial relations with every sector of society, well wishes for all, and then moving towards constructive growth in their respective fields. Their acts are compliant with the nation's development and strength, making them winners on every front in the entire world.

Citizens of a nation should devote their time to carrying out their duties without any favor and do more and more work instead of wasting their time on penny matters. Although such contributions may initially seem like little drops, they collectively turn into a big pond.

In my earlier book named "CHANAKYA OF MODERN BUSINESS GOVERNANCE & TIME MANAGEMENT," which relates to the area of business management, I have emphasized this approach even while one is engaged in carrying out business activities.

Our maximum concentration and focus should be to earn pounds even at the loss of pennies at times. If we talk in terms of ratios, in my opinion, 80% concentration should be on achieving the target level through pounds, and the balance concentration might be on pennies, which comes to 20% of the total energy, provided time is available to do such activities without compromising the effort to get pounds. A pound-wise approach is always considered best from either an earning point of view or savings in expenses. However, if time or other resources are available, then both can be considered either parallel or individually in a high-to-low value order.

A large number of examples can be quoted here for this topic, but even then, it would not turn out to be an exhaustive list, as everyone has his/her own experience. Furthermore, every entrepreneur understands the outcome of this approach, so I won't elaborate on this topic further. However, it has been observed that young entrants to business, whether male or female, use the penny-wise approach much more in business matters than the older generation. This may be due to the fact that elders might have gained experience from their long business tenure so far. Additionally, female entrepreneurs need to pay more attention to this approach. The English idiom "penny wise and pound foolish" is a popular saying that warns against safeguarding pennies while risking pounds—in other words, being stingy with small sums of money while being extravagant with larger sums.

Citizens of a nation are also supposed to devote their precious time to materialistic work. I have seen that many times they prefer to save a little by focusing on that job at the cost of their duties. This can be observed in areas such as house or building construction, caring for patients without any need, or wandering here and there just to buy things a bit cheaper, and so on. Even the need for improvement here cannot be denied, irrespective of the value.

Concept of Humanity – 21/4/2021

If we recall the time of the pandemic, which we all experienced, when medical and all other allied services were very limited, wherever the concept of humanity was followed in availing these facilities, the situation remained controlled and safe. Patients in dire need were given preference over those with less critical health problems when providing services such as hospital beds, oxygen, ventilators, medical staff, and others. A tough time passed due to such a kind spirit. More and more efforts are needed toward this.

Business Competition – 21/4/2021

Citizens in business should compete with cross-border entrepreneurs in manufacturing, service provision, or other commercial matters instead of focusing solely on their own countrymen. This is because the internal demand of a nation remains fixed at a time. If one entrepreneur cannot meet such demand, another is there to do so. But overall contribution remains the same, regardless of who has supplied the requirements. GDP would also remain the same. The only difference is that some more shares would go into the hands of one person instead of another. Thus, efforts should be targeted more towards outside demand.

Chapter 66

Informed Decision – Making by the People

The Significance of Public Awareness

The people of a country need to be smart in how they deal with various aspects of life. This intelligence should apply to everything, whether it's choosing government leaders, interacting with others in different situations, or grasping the policies and plans of the government and opposition parties. Having this intelligence helps people make the right decisions, select the right individuals for the nation's benefit, and make wise choices in their personal lives.

When people are smart in these ways, it ensures that the right people step forward to lead and manage various matters. This means that those in charge are well-qualified and knowledgeable. Furthermore, it reduces corruption, undue influence, and coercion in society over time.

Sometimes, we see individuals achieving high-profile positions, recognition, and opportunities because of their connections to politicians, bureaucrats, or through corrupt means. Meanwhile, others with more experience, qualifications, and a selfless approach can get left behind. This system of favoritism and corruption should come to an end in society.

A society where people understand the importance of making informed decisions and choose leaders based on their qualifications and abilities is a society that can progress and thrive. It is crucial for individuals to value competence and integrity over nepotism and corrupt practices. When people are well-informed and make choices that benefit the nation as a whole, everyone benefits, and society becomes fairer and more just.

Furthermore, promoting transparency in government and public life can help citizens make informed decisions and hold their leaders accountable. When people are aware of what is happening in their government and community, they can actively participate in shaping a better future for themselves and their nation.

Chapter 67

Having Realistic Expectations from The Government

Every citizen expects something from the government, either in the regular course of events or during the budget announcement. This is entirely reasonable because it is their right, and the government should actively work to meet these expectations. However, the key question is what kind of demands or expectations should be fulfilled. This is where the role of the public becomes crucial.

Sometimes, the public demands immediate benefits, even if it means the government has to borrow money from external sources or increase the fiscal deficit. They may want quick results, even if it means neglecting policies that would bring significant, long-lasting benefits in the future. For the sake of short-term gains, governments may make decisions that appeal to the public at the time but hinder constructive, long-term growth for both individuals and the nation.

For example, a government might announce tax benefits, such as lower income taxes, just before elections, making people feel like they have more money in their pockets compared to previous years. However, the government has to borrow extra money to cover these tax cuts. In the following year, to pay the interest on this extra borrowing and repay the borrowed amount, the government might have to impose various charges on the public, which could end up being more significant than the tax savings from the previous government. This is because interest payments on the extra borrowing increase over time.

SUMMARY

Citizens need to have realistic expectations from the government. While immediate benefits are appealing, it is crucial to consider the long-term consequences of government decisions. Sometimes, sacrificing short-term gains for sustainable, long-term growth is a more responsible approach. The government should also prioritize policies that benefit the nation as a whole in the long run rather than focusing solely on winning public favor in the short term. Public awareness and understanding of these trade-offs are essential for making informed decisions about government policies and budgets.

Chapter 68

Empower Women's Contribution

In the past, women didn't always get the recognition they deserved, but today, things have changed. Women are contributing in many ways, from leading in various fields to standing strong to protect their nations. It's clear that their work has an impact on a country's economic growth, so we shouldn't overlook their contributions.

In different parts of the world, women are competing with men in almost every aspect of life. Now, it's the government's responsibility to encourage them to keep participating for their own growth and that of the nation. Different countries may need different approaches based on factors like literacy rates and cultures. Some countries have made great progress in this area, but others still have work to do. Those lagging should spread awareness about the importance of women's contributions.

Apart from government efforts, society also plays a crucial role. Unfortunately, there are places where women are not given equal opportunities in education, sports, art, and sometimes even from birth. Is this advisable in today's world? Most people would likely disagree. We need to change our thinking and ensure that women have equal rights and opportunities as men in our society. We must prioritize areas where women are underrepresented.

According to reports available on the internet, women's participation in some countries is increasing, and that's a good sign. Even countries with less economic wealth can improve by promoting women's participation in the workforce. This can start with improving their health, education, and providing opportunities in administrative work, elections, and leadership roles over time. This will unlock their potential and bring diverse perspectives, experiences, and education to all aspects of society.

In countries where women already participate actively, their culture can serve as an example. A nation with a strong and balanced workforce, with both men and women contributing equally, gains a reputable position on the global stage.

The key is self-motivation. Women should be passionate about gaining education, participating in all aspects of life, and working alongside men. Their motivation will lead to positive changes on national and international levels. Over the years, we've seen women fighting for their rights and succeeding. Sooner or later, they achieve success in meeting their demands.

SUMMARY

Women play a vital role in shaping future generations, but this can only happen if they are self-reliant in all areas of life. Encouraging children, both boys and girls, to work hard and develop their intelligence is essential. There's no harm if girls engage in activities traditionally associated with boys in childhood and adolescence. This will help them gain courage, strength, and resilience, preparing them to face any challenges in life. Boys can also benefit from working alongside girls, fostering a sense of healthy competition and cooperation, making both genders stronger mentally and physically.

Chapter 69

The Role of Young Generation in Nation Building

Youngsters have a crucial role to play in shaping the future of a nation. Instead of simply indulging in indoor games, they should embrace a strong work ethic. This applies to both boys and girls, who should live their lives with determination and intelligence.

There's no harm, in my opinion, if girls live their lives with the same vigor as boys, from childhood to adolescence. Rather, the elders and social platforms should not make them understand the difference in gender up to a certain age limit. This way, girls would also undergo rigorous training. They can actively engage in work, whether it's at home, on farms, or even in tasks like cycling or driving. They can participate in the upkeep and maintenance of their national assets. By doing so, girls will gain courage, strength, and a resilient mindset that will help them overcome any challenges that come their way in life.

Boys, on the other hand, can benefit from healthy competition and cooperation with girls. Working alongside girls can motivate them to excel in various aspects of life. This collaboration can make both boys and girls mentally and physically stronger, preparing them for the responsibilities they will shoulder in the future.

SUMMARY

In summary, young people are the future of a nation, and their contributions are invaluable. By instilling a strong work ethic and encouraging equal participation from both genders, we can ensure that our youth actively contribute to building a prosperous and thriving nation.

Chapter 70

Sustainable Management of Population and Available Resources

Managing a Country's Population and Resources

When it comes to a country's population and its resources, we need to find a balance. Resources can be of two types: natural resources, which are gifts from nature like land, water, and minerals, and human-made resources created by the government and citizens. While having plenty of resources is great, they are not unlimited.

The people of a country are the ones who use these resources. The use of resources must be proportionate to what's available. This helps ensure that resources last longer and benefit everyone for a more extended period.

If resources are not used in proportion to their availability, problems can arise sooner or later. While we can produce some human-made resources, there are limits to what we can create due to various factors.

It's crucial to keep a country's population within a reasonable limit. While there may be some advantages to having a larger population, it's generally better to have a population that matches the available resources. This way, we can avoid overusing resources and ensure sustainability for the future.

Population management and resource sustainability are critical aspects of a country's long-term well-being. When a country's population grows too rapidly and consumes resources at an unsustainable rate, it can lead to environmental degradation and resource scarcity. Finding the right balance between population size and available resources is essential for the prosperity and sustainability of a nation. This often involves considering factors such as family planning, education, and responsible resource management.

To further elaborate on the concept of providing suggestions, implementing a system that regularly updates information on the accessibility of essential resources, calculates the per capita demand for these resources, identifies any shortfalls in the supply-demand ratio, and disseminates alerts to the public regarding precautionary measures and health concerns can significantly contribute to raising awareness among the populace. This heightened awareness can play a pivotal role in controlling the alarming rise in population growth. It serves as an instrumental means to strike a balance between the availability of critical resources and the ever-growing demand for them.

This initiative becomes especially crucial in under-privileged or low-income communities, such as slum areas, where access to resources may be limited. In such areas, the involvement of Non-Governmental Organizations (NGOs) can be invaluable in carrying out awareness campaigns and facilitating the necessary steps to address resource scarcity and overpopulation. NGO services can prove highly effective in spearheading these awareness initiatives, thus fostering a more sustainable and equitable future.

Chapter 71

Prioritizing Earned Income Over Speculative or Easy Gains

Citizens need to focus on earning money through their hard work rather than relying on speculative or easy income. For instance, instead of concentrating on making money through property investments, stock markets, or commodities like metal, copper, or nickel, people should emphasize building their income through consistent efforts.

When individuals rely too much on speculative income, they often become overconfident and disconnected from reality. This can lead to negative feelings among those who earn their income through hard work. They may start feeling disinterested in their jobs and believe that they can never compete with speculative earners. As a result, they might lose the motivation to progress and limit their earning potential. However, the fact is that hard-earned income always fosters sustained growth both for individuals and for the nation.

Building a nation requires a strong and motivated workforce. When citizens prioritize hard-earned income, it not only promotes a healthier work ethic but also contributes to the overall development of the country. Hard work, dedication, and consistent efforts are essential for personal growth and the prosperity of the nation. Encouraging individuals to value the importance of earning through their labor and skills can lead to a more robust and sustainable economy.

Chapter 72

Financial Literacy and Wise Management of Personal Income

Everyone must use their income wisely. In a nation, there should be a record of how much money each person earns.

When people manage their income wisely, it benefits both them and the country. Wise financial choices can lead to personal growth and a stable economy for the nation. A financially intelligent person can face the worst situations and overcome difficult times. It saddens me greatly when I learn that someone has committed suicide due to financial distress, non-repayment of borrowings, or an inability to receive medical treatment.

Effective financial management is essential for personal and national development. When individuals make informed decisions about their income, such as saving, investing, and spending responsibly, it contributes to their financial well-being. On a national level, having accurate records of citizens' income can help governments plan and implement policies that support economic growth and social welfare programs. Encouraging financial literacy and responsible money management is a valuable step toward building a prosperous nation.

Chapter 73

Building the Nation through Hard Work and Enjoying Life

We should work as long as we can and enjoy life along the way, without setting a fixed retirement age for ourselves.

By staying active and engaged in work and life, we not only benefit ourselves but also contribute to the betterment of our nation. Our experience and expertise can be valuable assets for the country. So, let's keep working and savoring life's moments without feeling obligated to retire at a certain age.

Chapter 74

The Role of Media in Building a Nation

Imagine a nation as a big puzzle and each person in the country is a piece of that puzzle. The media is like a messenger that helps people understand what's happening around them. It's like the news on TV, in newspapers, and online platforms.

When the media does its job honestly, it's like giving everyone the right puzzle pieces. They inform people about important things like what the government is doing, what's happening in different parts of the country, and how people are living their lives. This information helps everyone understand the big picture of the nation. When people know what's going on, they can make good decisions about how to help their country grow and become better. They can vote for leaders who care about them and their needs. They can also see problems and work together to find solutions.

Due to these reasons, the responsibility of the media becomes crucial to a nation and its people. They need to tell the truth and share accurate information with loyalty and honesty towards their duties. Just like how a good friend shows the real picture and doesn't spread rumors or say things that could cause fights, the media should avoid spreading false or harmful information.

To show the real facts happening in society is deemed to be the prime duty of the media without any coercion or influence.

Media plays a crucial role in shaping modern society. It serves as the primary channel through which information, ideas, and opinions are disseminated to the masses. Over the years, the media landscape has evolved significantly, with the advent of digital platforms enabling real-time news updates, social networking, and interactive content. In this context, the role of media becomes increasingly relevant, influencing various aspects of society, including politics, culture, education, and public opinion.

The news that creates chaos in a particular category of people should be interpreted in such a way that a wrong message is not conveyed while keeping the truth intact. To help maintain peace and good relationships, the media can show stories of people from different backgrounds working together and being kind to each other. This helps everyone see that we're all part of the same community, despite our differences.

SUMMARY

The role of media in modern society is multifaceted and influential. As a powerful agent of information dissemination, it has a profound impact on public opinion, culture, and democratic processes. With this power comes the responsibility to maintain journalistic integrity, uphold unbiased reporting, and contribute positively to the betterment of society. As consumers of media, individuals should also exercise critical thinking and media literacy to navigate the vast and diverse media landscape in an informed manner.

E. Judicial Reforms

Delayed justice loses its glory as it diminishes the impact of punishment and allows criminals to benefit from the leniency of the courts. To address this issue, the practice of 'date after date' (*tareekh-pe-tareekh*) in legal decisions needs to be eliminated.

Chapter 75

Upholding the Rule of Law

To ensure things are in proper order, having a fear of the law is really important. This is especially true in today's world, where people find new ways to break the law. Before I talk more about how people feel scared of the law, let's consider the country's Constitution. The Constitution is like a rulebook for the country.

The rules in the law should be strong enough to ensure people follow them and that everything stays peaceful. This means that the law should be strict (but fair according to societal conditions). If someone wants to break the law, they should be afraid of getting punished. If there's no punishment, nobody would care about the law. For example, if a person commits a serious crime like murder and the punishment for such a crime is not decided for a long time—such as more than 30 years—and when finally decided, the punishment is only one year, then people won't take the law seriously.

Similarly, people who play a vital role in spreading anti-national ideas among the public should also receive strong punishments, such as long prison sentences.

When it comes to maintaining a peaceful and orderly society, the fear of consequences outlined by the law plays a crucial role. In today's dynamic world, where creative ways of breaking the rules can emerge, instilling a sense of fear regarding legal repercussions becomes paramount.

Before delving further into the fear that the general population might have regarding the law, it's essential to spotlight the significance of a country's Constitution. This legal framework serves as the bedrock of a nation's rules and regulations.

The effectiveness of laws lies in their ability to command respect through appropriate strictness, tailored to fit societal conditions. The fear of facing punishment should deter individuals from entertaining the notion of breaking the law. This aspect gains prominence when considering cases where serious crimes like murder linger in legal limbo for extended periods, with inadequate penalties that fail to convey the gravity of the offense. Such instances undermine the authority of the law and diminish the inherent fear that should accompany its breach.

कठोर सजा में कमी अपराधों के बढ़ने का सबसे बड़ा कारण : शांता कुमार

पालमपुर, 31 दिसम्बर (ब्यूरो): पूर्व मुख्यमंत्री शांता कुमार ने कहा कि शिमला उच्च न्यायालय ने सोलन के आकाश की फांसी की सजा को उम्रकैद में बदल दिया। पूरा समाचार पढ़कर मैं दुखी भी हुआ, हैरान भी हुआ और आहत हो गया। 7 वर्ष की एक मासूम बच्ची का आकाश ने अपहरण किया था। इसके बाद उससे बलात्कार किया और फिर बड़ी बेरहमी से उसकी गला घोंट कर हत्या कर दी।

शांता कुमार ने कहा कि इतना ही नहीं दरिंदगी की सारी हदें पार करते हुए उस 7 साल की मासूम बच्ची के प्राइवेट पार्ट में लकड़ी का टुकड़ा भी डाला था। सोलन के न्यायालय ने इसे घोर अपराध कहा था और फांसी की सजा सुनाई थी। उच्च न्यायालय ने अपने फैसले में कहा कि यह अपराध रेयर ऑफ रेयररैस्ट का मामला नहीं बनता। मुझे पढ़कर बहुत हैरानी हुई।

उन्होंने कहा कि पहला अपराध 7 साल की मासूम बेटी का अपहरण किया, दूसरा अपराध उससे बलात्कार किया, तीसरा अपराध उसका गला घोंट कर हत्या कर दी और चौथा अपराध उसके प्राइवेट पार्ट में लकड़ी का टुकड़ा डाला।

उस दरिंदे ने और कौन सा अपराध नहीं किया जिसके कारण उसके अपराध को रेयर ऑफ रेयररैस्ट कहा जाए और कुछ करने के लिए बचा ही नहीं था इसलिए सोलन की अदालत ने उसे फांसी की सजा दी थी।

Instances Reflecting Legal Inconsistencies

The justice system can sometimes leave us puzzled due to its inconsistencies and varying outcomes. These cases exemplify the disparities within legal decisions and the impact they can have on societal perceptions.

An example of such inhumanity is the case of a seven-year-old girl who was kidnapped, raped, and murdered by her assailant. The brutality of the attack, including acts of torture beyond comprehension, shocked the nation. The criminal committed acts beyond human comprehension, torturing her by inserting a wooden piece into her private part before killing her.

This culprit was sentenced to death by the District Court. The decision was met with widespread public approval. However, the High Court commuted this sentence to life imprisonment, arguing that the case did not meet the criteria for the "rarest of rare" category, thus making the death penalty inappropriate. I question what more the criminal could have done to be considered worthy of the death penalty in the eyes of the court. With such leniency in the law, can we truly expect a day when the country is free from such heinous crimes? I can confidently assert on behalf of everyone that the answer is unequivocally NO.

In a similar case in a country where a senior person died in a road rage incident involving a politician, the punishment came after 34 years by the Supreme Court of that country in a reconsideration verdict of a fine of Rs. 1000, approximately 12/13 USD. This punishment was for only one year.

On the contrary, there are examples of some countries where laws are not only strict but also applied equally for all, regardless of their status. Mr. Boris Johnson, a former Prime Minister of Britain, reported that Rishi Sunak, the current Prime Minister of the same country, was fined in January 2023 for not fastening his seat belt while traveling and interviewing a reporter. I learned that he was actually wearing his seat belt, but when the interview started, he removed it, thinking that it might look unappealing to viewers on TV. Until the interview was aired, no one noticed that he was without a belt. It was only when the opposition raised their voice about a Prime Minister violating traveling rules that the police took immediate action and found him without a seat belt.

Can we ever expect to witness such an incident in our country involving MPs, MLAs, or other politicians, let alone the Prime Minister?

Extending this concept, it's imperative that those who actively propagate harmful ideologies contrary to the nation's interests also face substantial penalties. By holding such individuals accountable and subjecting them to significant legal consequences, a message is sent that the law is steadfast and resolute, further emphasizing the importance of upholding societal order through the fear of the law in upholding societal order.

Chapter 76

Strengthening Investigative Agencies

Understanding Investigating Agencies and Their Impact

Investigating agencies can be divided into two main categories: financial and non-financial. These agencies lose their credibility if the people responsible for their work are not honest and loyal. They are responsible for looking into various kinds of cases, which includes questioning people, searching for evidence, and confiscating things that are related to the case. They play a big role in identifying those responsible for illegal activities and accusing them of those actions. Unfortunately, some dishonest individuals misuse these agencies for their own gain. They ignore cases involving money that should go to the government, whether it's the State, Central, or Local Government. When this becomes common, these agencies become ineffective and a waste of resources for the government.

There is a specific focus on financial investigations in this context. These investigations only benefit the government by about 20%. The rest of the benefits are lost due to various reasons. If these investigations were carried out more effectively, the government could earn a lot more money.

Referring to a news article from Punjab Kesari dated July 29, 2022, in the "Off The Record" column, some important data was shared. Over a five-year period, there were 3,787 cases of Income Tax investigation involving big companies and wealthy individuals. Out of these, only 1,956 cases, which is about half, led to legal actions. In this time frame (2017-2022), only 29 cases resulted in punishments, and properties worth 5,890 Crore Rupees were seized. It is not mentioned how much of this seized property actually translated into additional tax revenue, penalties, and interest payments, as all the seized property generally does not get adjusted against tax, penalty, or interest, but is released against the production of evidence.

Without clear details, assuming that the seized property directly translates to revenue, the Income Tax Department's total revenue would be around 1.5 Crore Rupees per case. This seems like a small amount when considering the huge economy of 3,000 billion USD. It raises questions about whether the expenses incurred in these investigations, including staff salaries, infrastructure, and other costs, are worth the relatively modest returns of around 1,200 Crore Rupees per year or 100 Crore Rupees per month.

This is just one department's case, and there are many other similar situations in different departments. Investigating agencies serve as vital instruments in upholding justice and accountability within a society. Their effectiveness is highly contingent on the integrity and dedication of those entrusted with their operation. Split into financial and non-financial spheres, these agencies maintain their significance by ensuring adherence to rules and regulations.

Financial investigations, in particular, hold the potential to bolster a nation's revenue streams significantly. However, the execution of these investigations demands precision and transparency.

A key concern lies in the efficacy of converting seized assets into tangible financial gains for the government, as not all seized property directly correlates with monetary liabilities.

The mentioned news article highlights the complex landscape of investigative outcomes. In five years, a considerable number of cases underwent scrutiny, yet the number of resulting legal actions remains modest. The limited number of successful prosecutions, coupled with the seized property's ambiguous monetary contribution, underscores the need for enhanced clarity and streamlined processes.

Considering the vast economic context, the revenue generated from investigations raises questions about its adequacy, especially in contrast to the substantial expenses incurred in maintaining the investigative machinery. This instance serves as a microcosm of broader systemic challenges that necessitate careful analysis and reform across various departments and agencies.

Final Thoughts

The effectiveness of investigating agencies is crucial not only in terms of financial outcomes but also for maintaining public trust. If these agencies end up costing more than the revenue they generate, it's sensible to consider their closure. This step not only makes financial sense but also curbs potential debates and controversies surrounding their operations, preserving the agencies' integrity.

In the fight against financial misconduct, adopting strategies like those outlined in Chapter 11 to address "Black Money" offers a pathway for navigating complex challenges. Incorporating such approaches into decision-making processes could pave the way for a more transparent and accountable investigative framework.

Chapter 77

Role and Challenges of Police & Security Forces

In order to maintain law and order, the duties of the first line of responders become the key factor for the effective results. In the earlier times, our police personnel were supposed to be physically strong to control various situations and instill fear in the minds of the residents. But as technology has advanced, the ways of committing crimes have taken a new shape, which requires the updating of our officers to the latest crime techniques and cyber expertise. Today, attacks are carried out using intelligence or new technology rather than primarily through physical assaults.

Sensitivity is another quality that a country's local police must possess to effectively resolve cases of disputes between individuals. Although cruel offenders do not deserve such treatment, for others, this will help in winning their confidence in the security forces. In the prisons of a country, the culture should be such that promotes sensitive thinking, particularly for those prisoners who are involved in cruelty, riots, hate speeches, and anti-national activities.

A comprehensive approach to incarceration involves fostering a culture of empathy, particularly for inmates involved in severe crimes and anti-social activities. This does not diminish the gravity of their actions but aims to encourage introspection and rehabilitation, ultimately contributing to a safer and more empathetic society.

This does not imply that security forces should not possess physical strength. On the contrary, it is essential that they remain physically strong. Particularly when dealing with minor or non-technical crimes, social riots, or similar issues, the presence of security personnel can instill fear and deter crime. If a thief or jewelry snatcher does not fear the presence of a policeman and continues their activities believing they are stronger than the police officer, this perception needs to be changed. A security officer must be suitably trained to handle at least two or three people to maintain a sense of authority and fear among culprits. Even in routine tasks such as traffic control, inspections, and other duties, the impression of physical strength plays a very vital role in maintaining law and resolving various issues.

Chapter 78

Designated Areas for Immoral Activities

If there is persistent interest among people in such activities, it may be better to provide a separate area for them to keep the rest of society clean. The concept of creating designated areas for immoral activities has been a topic of debate for some time. Proponents argue that providing such spaces could regulate and control these activities, leading to greater transparency and reduced corruption. However, this proposal raises ethical, moral, and practical questions about the role of government in regulating personal behavior and the consequences for society as a whole.

The decision to implement such a policy should involve a thorough examination of societal values, legal frameworks, and the potential impact on the well-being of the nation's citizens. It is essential to strike a balance between regulating activities to protect society and respecting individual rights and cultural values. Any policy in this regard must take into consideration the interests of all parties involved and consider the consequences for the nation's social fabric, ethics, and long-term development.

The idea of allocating separate areas for immoral activities within a nation's framework has sparked debates and discussions for years.

Proponents of this thought argue that providing designated spaces for such activities can help maintain social order and protect public morals. However, this concept is not without its ethical, legal, and social challenges. This essay examines the concept of creating separate areas for immoral activities in the context of nation-building, exploring its potential advantages and drawbacks.

Advantages

1. Social Order and Control

Proponents argue that allocating separate spaces for immoral activities, such as gambling or adult entertainment, can help regulate and control these industries. By confining these activities to designated areas, governments can implement stricter regulations, enforce age restrictions, and monitor for illegal practices. This can reduce the negative impact of such activities on wider society.

2. Tax Revenue

Some proponents also point out the potential economic benefits. Taxation of immoral activities within designated areas can generate significant revenue for the government. This revenue can be channeled into public services, infrastructure development, or social welfare programs, contributing to the nation's overall development.

Drawbacks

1. Ethical and Moral Concerns

One of the most significant criticisms of this concept is its ethical and moral implications. It raises questions about whether a society should endorse or facilitate activities that are considered immoral by a significant portion of its population. This approach may conflict with the cultural and moral values of many citizens.

2. Social Stigmatization

Designating separate areas for immoral activities may lead to the stigmatization of those involved in these activities. It could create a marginalized and vulnerable community, potentially increasing the risks associated with these activities.

3. Legal and Regulatory Challenges

Implementing and regulating such designated areas can pose significant legal and administrative challenges. Ensuring compliance with regulations, preventing illegal activities, and addressing issues related to public safety and health may become complex tasks.

4. Potential for Corruption

Designated areas may become breeding grounds for corruption if not managed effectively. Corruption within regulatory bodies can undermine the intended benefits and perpetuate illegal practices and crimes.

SUMMARY

The concept of allocating separate areas for immoral activities within a nation's framework remains a highly contentious and complex issue. While proponents argue that it can help maintain social order, generate revenue, and control these activities, there are significant ethical, moral, and practical challenges to consider.

Chapter 79

Uniform Legal System

To address disagreements and biases among the people of a country, it is suggested to have a single law that applies to everyone, especially when there are differences in caste, occupation, wealth, and more. This way, no particular group would feel unfairly treated by the government, and unnecessary conflicts would definitely decrease. In some countries, this does not happen, leading to ongoing disturbances caused by different groups of citizens. These disruptions can halt development progress and waste national resources, adversely affecting various sectors, including the government and the general public.

We can imagine how much time and focus are wasted with little or no output. Public resources go to waste, and each sector bears its adverse effects, whether it is the government or the public, both those in favor and those against, at a particular point.

A huge agitation, whether in one way or another, cannot be denied, particularly when there are numerous regions, castes, and religions. However, to the maximum extent possible, all the varied classes of people should come under the umbrella of a single law. In very few religious cases, exceptions may be necessary, and these should be clear, concise, and precise without any discrimination.

SUMMARY

To ensure a smooth and fulfilling life for citizens, a universal law can be highly beneficial. However, a subcategory of laws within the main law, may not be denied up to a limit.

Chapter 80

Expedited Legal Processes

Delayed justice loses its glory as it diminishes the impact of punishment and allows criminals to benefit from the leniency of the courts. To address this issue, the practice of 'date after date' (*tareekh-pe-tareekh*) in legal decisions needs to be eliminated.

Slow decision-making in legal cases is detrimental to everyone involved, including the courts, disputing parties, and legal counsels. Such delays can lead to:

1. Slowed administrative work and hindered improvements in court operations that could have been achieved if case pendency were reduced.
2. Misuse of financial resources allocated for running the courts, whether visible or hidden.
3. Loss of faith in the judicial system, which can have detrimental psychological effects on the public.

To tackle these problems, Hon'ble judges can manage proceedings more efficiently by allowing reasonable time and restricting adjournments at each stage of the process for each case, ensuring that hearings are constructive, and optimizing working hours.

To address this backlog, courts can promote arbitration proceedings, when possible, at a lower fee.

Verdicts/Reports – Size and Clarity

Keep legal language simple to aid common understanding. It has often been observed that investigating agencies or court verdicts span hundreds or even thousands of pages, raising several concerns:

- Are such lengthy reports truly necessary in all cases?
- Does each word of the content add unique meaning, or is there unnecessary repetition?
- Could the whole content be summarized more succinctly
- Would an ordinary person be able to comprehend such reports without the specialized knowledge of those making the decisions?

Authorities should consider these aspects and aim for more concise reports. Additionally, legal language should be simplified to make it more comprehensible for the general public.

Chapter 81

Promoting Spiritualism and Cultivating Gentle Behavior for National Harmony and Progress

In an increasingly interconnected and complex world, fostering a culture of spiritualism and gentle behavior within society, including within the government, can have profound implications for national harmony, progress, and global peace. This proposal aims to outline the functioning, advantages, and potential disadvantages of spreading spiritualism and gentle behavior across all sections of society, focusing on mitigating internal conflicts and contributing to global stability.

Promoting spiritualism and gentle behavior involves a multifaceted approach that incorporates teachings on empathy, tolerance, and mindfulness into educational curricula at all levels. Encouraging understanding and respect for diverse beliefs and cultures would further this goal. The government should lead by example, emphasizing ethical leadership, transparency, and accountability. Public servants should undergo training to foster a culture of service, compassion, and fairness.

Additionally, community-based programs, dialogues, and activities that facilitate interfaith and intercultural understanding should be encouraged. Promoting discussions and forums to address grievances and concerns peacefully is also essential.

The role of media and communication remains crucial in today's world. Encouraging responsible reporting and media practices that highlight positive stories of unity, cooperation, and shared values helps promote gentle behavior as a social norm.

The adoption of spiritualism and gentle behavior offers numerous advantages:

Conflict Mitigation: Fostering tolerance and empathy can reduce the likelihood of internal conflicts, communal tensions, and violence.

Social Cohesion: Encouraging gentle behavior nurtures a sense of belonging and unity among diverse groups within society.

Global Image: A nation that promotes spiritualism and gentle behavior gains a positive international reputation, potentially reducing conflicts and enhancing diplomatic relations.

Economic Progress: A harmonious society is more conducive to economic growth and development. Businesses thrive in an environment of peace and stability.

Moral Leadership: By taking a principled stand for peace and cooperation, a nation can serve as a beacon of moral leadership on the global stage.

Disadvantages

While the benefits are compelling, there are potential disadvantages:

Resistance to Change: Implementing changes in

education, governance, and societal norms may face resistance from traditionalist or extremist factions.

Resource Allocation: Initiatives to promote spiritualism and gentle behavior may require significant financial and administrative resources, potentially diverting attention from other pressing issues.

Complexity of Implementation: Cultural, religious, and regional diversity can complicate efforts to create a universal approach to spiritualism and gentle behavior.

Long-Term Commitment: Achieving widespread adoption of spiritualism and gentle behavior is a long-term process that requires sustained commitment from all stakeholders.

SUMMARY

In conclusion, the promotion of spiritualism and gentle behavior across society, including within the government, is a laudable objective with far-reaching benefits for national and global well-being. It is essential to recognize the potential challenges and complexities involved in implementing these changes. However, the potential to reduce internal conflicts, enhance Social cohesion and contribution to global peace and prosperity makes the pursuit of these ideals a worthy endeavor. Through education, leadership and community engagement, nations can create a more harmonious and peaceful world.

Message to the Readers

Dear Readers,

It is with great pleasure and a deep sense of purpose that I present to you this book on the art and science of nation-building. In a world brimming with complexities and challenges, the task of shaping a prosperous, harmonious, and just society can seem daunting. Yet, it is precisely in these challenges that we find the opportunity to create something extraordinary.

This book is the culmination of years of research, analysis, and reflection, and it is my sincere hope that it serves as a guiding light on your journey toward understanding the intricate tapestry of nationhood. Building a nation is not merely the responsibility of leaders or policymakers; it is a collective endeavor that requires the active participation and commitment of every citizen.

As you embark on this exploration of the principles, strategies, and ideals that underpin nation-building, I encourage you to approach these pages with an open mind and a willingness to engage in thoughtful discourse. The path to building a nation is not set in stone; it is a dynamic process that evolves with the times and the aspirations of its people.

While this book offers insights and strategies, it is ultimately up to you, the reader, to apply and adapt these ideas to your unique circumstances. I invite you to question, discuss, and debate the concepts presented here, for it is through dialogue and collaboration that we refine our understanding and approach to nation-building.

I am deeply grateful for your interest in this crucial topic and for your commitment to making a positive impact on your nation and the world. Together, we can work towards a future where nations thrive in unity, diversity, and prosperity.

Thank you for joining me on this journey. May your efforts in building a better nation be guided by wisdom, compassion, and a vision of a brighter tomorrow.

Warm regards,

(R. Kumar)

Glimpses

- Erroneous decisions made by a government can plunge the nation into darkness, while wise choices illuminate its path to global acclaim.
- Principle of a balanced approach between our values and those of others should be taken care of.
- To make a friend takes time, but to make an enemy might not take long.
- Opposition parties should also recognize when to support initiatives that are genuinely beneficial for the nation. Similarly, the ruling party should address opposition concerns with transparency and factual information.
- Efforts are being made to soften the news without changing its original purpose or sometimes ignored.
- Decentralization of official powers may prove to be a milestone towards the elimination of corruption.
- Opening of Evening Offices (through Private Agencies) by Government Departments for Public Convenience
- We cannot conceal the rays of light forever. Sooner or later, they will shine."
- Bribery is an insect that eats away justice and revenue of the government.
- To further elaborate on the concept of providing suggestions, implementing a system that regularly updates information on the accessibility of essential

resources, calculates the per capita demand for these resources, identifies any shortfalls in the supply-demand ratio, and disseminates alerts to the public regarding precautionary measures and health concerns can significantly contribute to raising awareness among the populace. This heightened awareness can play a pivotal role in controlling the alarming rise in population growth. It serves as an instrumental means to strike a balance between the availability of critical resources and the ever-growing demand for them. This initiative becomes especially crucial in underprivileged or low-income communities, such as slum areas, where access to resources may be limited.

- Work during Pension period by the Retirees - "If it's not deemed suitable for an entire retirement, at the very least, this practice should continue for the first ten years. Comparatively, in the private sector, entrepreneurs often work well into their 80s and even 90s. Therefore, there is no reason why the government sector shouldn't consider a similar approach."
- In general, I don't oppose a government's charitable efforts to uplift disadvantaged segments of society. However, providing assistance should be a reciprocal process, encouraging individuals to contribute in return. This not only stimulates the pursuit of additional avenues for income but also ensures the judicious use of limited resources in areas that might not be of utmost importance. Nevertheless, the notion of unconditionally receiving without any corresponding effort may not serve the long-term interests of the deserving beneficiaries. Hence, if something is provided without any cost, there should be an accompanying expectation of engagement in productive activities. This approach helps prevent

the development of a habit of non-productivity and encourages a sense of responsibility and contribution to the nation.

- Keep the responsibilities of government staff intact even after retirement for the work they carried out during their tenure. If any lapse is found in their role, disciplinary action should be taken.
- Government departments that are particularly susceptible to this form of corruption could categorize public work into two distinct classes. The first category would involve the standard process, while the second category would be designated as 'Special,' with an associated extra fee.
- Delayed justice loses its glory as it diminishes the impact of punishment and allows criminals to benefit from the leniency of the courts. To address this issue, the practice of 'date after date' (*tareekh pe tareekh*) in legal decisions needs to be eliminated.

End

In the end, as we conclude this book, I want to express my heartfelt gratitude to you, dear reader. Your commitment to learning and dedication to the noble endeavor of nation-building are truly inspiring.

Remember that this book is just the beginning of your journey. Building a nation is a dynamic and ongoing process, and the true test lies in the actions you take beyond these pages. Your passion, vision, and determination will be the driving forces behind the transformation of your nation.

Always keep in mind that nation-building is a collective effort. It thrives on the diverse talents, ideas, and energies of its citizens. Embrace the diversity within your nation, for it is the wellspring of innovation and progress.

Never lose sight of the values that underpin a just and prosperous society: equality, justice, empathy, and resilience. These are the pillars upon which great nations are built.

I encourage you to share the knowledge and insights you've gained from this book with others. Engage in dialogue, foster understanding, and collaborate with fellow citizens to create a brighter future together.

Nation-building is not without its challenges, but it is through overcoming these challenges that we truly grow and evolve. Believe in the potential of your nation and never underestimate the impact your actions can have on shaping its destiny.

In closing, I wish you all the best on your journey to build a nation that reflects your highest ideals and aspirations. May your efforts create a legacy of prosperity, unity, and enduring greatness.

With deepest appreciation,

R. Kumar

Disclaimer

The views expressed in this book are those of the author(s) and do not necessarily reflect the views of any other individuals or organizations, except from some references from news sources and other types of communication, including newspapers and media. The content of this book is not intended to target any specific nation, class, creed, workforce, citizens, staff, or personal sentiments of anyone. It is meant to present ideas in general terms. If anyone feels unintentionally hurt by any part of the book due to personal opinions or sentiments, I sincerely apologize for the same.

